A1

Olive Green
English

The authors of film dialogues and vocabulary lists: Wojciech Wojtasiak,
Magdalena Warżała-Wojtasiak

The authors of grammar: Marta Borowiak-Dostatnia (A1-B1), Marcin Mortka (B2-C1)

The authors of interactive dialogues and vocabulary lists: Marta Borowiak-Dostatnia,
Monika Glińska

Proofreading: Monika Glińska, Alicja Jankowiak, Natalia Wajda

Edited by: Alicja Jankowiak

Recordings: Graham Crawford, Joanna Haracz-Lewandowska, Jagoda Lembicz,
Dale Taylor, Marianna Waters-Sobkowiak

Cover design: Marcin Stanisławski

Graphic design and composition: Wioletta Kowalska / Violet Design

Stock photos: © Fotolia.com

Olive Green English A1

Publisher Chung Kyudo

Editors Cho Sangik, Hong Inpyo, Kim Taeyeon, Kwak Bitna

Designers Kim Nakyung, Yoon Hyunjoo, Im Miyoung

First Published January 2018
By Darakwon Bldg., 211, Munbal-ro, Paju-si, Gyeonggi-do 10881, Republic of Korea
Tel. 82-2-736-2031 (Ext. 550-553)

© Copyright SuperMemo World sp. z o.o., 2018
   SuperMemo is the registered trademark by SuperMemo World sp. z o.o.

© Copyright for the South Korean edition by Darakwon, 2018

All rights reserved. No part of this publication may be reproduced, stored in a retrieval system,
or transmitted in any form or by any means, electronic, mechanical, photocopying, or otherwise,
without the prior consent of the copyright owner. Refund after purchase is possible only according
to the company regulations. Contact the above telephone number for any inquiries.
Consumer damages caused by loss, damage, etc. can be compensated according to the consumer
dispute resolution standards announced by the Korea Fair Trade Commission.
An incorrectly collated book will be exchanged.

Price ₩12,000
ISBN: 978-89-277-0951-0 14740
          978-89-277-0950-3 14740 (set)

http://www.darakwon.co.kr
Main Book / Free MP3 Available Online
9 8 7 6 5 4 3   20 21 22 23 24

Table of contents

Introduction 4

Scene 1: Job offer you can't refuse 8
Personal pronouns • to be • Possessive pronouns • Articles
Introducing yourself • Providing basic information about yourself (nationality, age, profession, phone number, address, e-mail)

Scene 2: Meet the Murrays 18
Demonstrative pronouns • have got • Saxon genitive
Describing your family • Formulating simple questions • Asking for more information • Encouraging dialogue

Scene 3: Old Berry's best B&B 26
Present Simple (structure and uses)
Greetings and goodbyes • Booking a hotel room • Checking in at the hotel • Opening hours, e.g. of a hotel restaurant

Scene 4: Awkward supper 34
Present Simple (questions, short answers) • Expressing preferences • gerund
Planning for the afternoon • Preparing meals • Sport as a leisure activity

Scene 5: Jogging in the park 42
there is/are • Prepositions • Articles
Going on a date • Planning for an evening out together • Describing the town and choosing your transport

Scene 6: Don't date in the pub! 50
Past Simple • Question words • would like to
Booking a table • Ordering food and drinks

Scene 7: Campbell Manor 58
Past Simple • Comparative adjectives
Showing a guest around the house • Sharing family stories • Describing the members of your family

Scene 8: Let's plan this theft 68
can/can't (abilities) • Prepositions of movement
Going out with friends • Inviting a friend to the cinema, a concert or a party

Scene 9: Olive goes shopping for a dress 76
Present Continuous
At the grocer's and in a newsagents • Shopping for clothes and shoes

Scene 10: Party time 86
will
Giving advice about health and lifestyle • Asking for help • Describing your health and general state

Scene 11: It's time to steal...something 94
Present Perfect • Present Perfect vs. Past Simple • Imperative forms
Organising a meeting or an event • Giving orders • Planning your actions • Justifying your point of view

Scene 12: Run! 104
have to • can/can't (prohibition) • must
Traffic rules and road signs • Means of transport • Using electronic devices such as satnav

Translation 114

Introduction

Olive Green is an innovative course for those who want to learn English from the beginning in a way that is both modern and efficient. It is the perfect combination of fun and effective learning of the highest order.

The **Olive Green** multimedia course is based on an **interactive action film**, where you can decide what course the plot will take, as well as play some arcade-type and language games. The course is divided into 12 film scenes for each language skill level.

What is the best way to learn with the **Olive Green** course?

To begin with, watch the right **film scene** in the multimedia course. We encourage you to watch it several times, so that you can gradually get used to the natural pronunciation you hear and make decisions during interactions. The **subtitles** (available in English and many other languages) will help you understand the content of the dialogue. If you are learning English from scratch, first watch each scene with subtitles in your own language (if available), then with English subtitles, and finally without subtitles. Next, read the **text of the film dialogue** in the book. Then listen to the MP3 recordings of the dialogue, and lastly try to read the text aloud.

Each scene in the book is accompanied by a **list of new words and expressions**. Read them and find them in the dialogue to see how they are used in context, and then listen to the recording of the list.

In the next step, please read the **grammar explanations** describing the most important topics introduced in each film dialogue. You will find many examples of typical applications of all the new structures in these sections.

The multimedia course also includes **interactive dialogues** to let you practice in a variety of communication situations and develop the skills necessary for a conversation in English. Additionally, selected variants of these dialogues have been included in the book, together with the lists of new words and phrases that will help you expand your vocabulary for each topic.

Last but not least, read the **cultural commentary** that will introduce you to some interesting aspects of the culture of the English-speaking countries. The language of the commentaries is simple, but if you are just starting your adventure with English, it may be hard to understand. In that case, please remember that it is always better to try to analyze and understand the general meaning of any English text on your own first – especially if you have been working with the course for some time. Consulting a dictionary for definitions or equivalents of the words that may be new to you should generally be your "second best" option.

To those who wish to continue learning English with **Olive Green**, we recommend the rest part of the course at the other levels.

Enjoy your learning!
The SuperMemo World team
& Darakwon Olive Green team

Olive Green

level A1

Scene 1

Film dialogue and vocabulary

Read the dialogue between an assistant (A) and his client (C). Check the list of words and phrases below.

Her full name is Gabriella Aguilar. A-G-U-I-L-A-R.

A: Nationality: American. Age: 26. She is a very talented art thief. Her boss is Dieter Kirsch, but things are complicated between them now and there is a price on her head. She is alone and broke. In my opinion, she is perfect!

C: She's so young … but okay!

Vocabulary

full name	(생략하지 않은) 성명	complicated	복잡한
nationality	국적	now	지금
American	미국인의; 미국인	price on one's head	수배자 현상금
age	나이	alone	혼자인
very	매우, 몹시	broke	무일푼의, 빈털터리의
talented	유능한, 재능 있는	in one's opinion	~의 생각에는
art	미술품	perfect	최적의, 완벽한
thief	절도범, 도둑	young	어린, 젊은
boss	보스, 두목	Okay!	좋아!, 알았어!
things	상황, 사정, 형편		

level A1

Read the dialogue between the client (C) and Gabriella (G). Check the list of words and phrases below.

C: Ms Aguilar – an art … what's the word?
G: Consultant. I'm an art consultant.
C: Consultant? Yes, that's very funny! Well, I'm your new client. A new client with a great job offer.

Vocabulary				
	word	단어, 낱말	new	새로운
	consultant	컨설턴트	great	정말 좋은
	Yes.	그래.., 맞아.	job	일자리, 일
	funny	재미있는, 우스운	job offer	일자리 제의

What should Gabriella do?

accept

don't accept

G: All right! What's the job?
C: It's easy and it's in the UK.
G: UK? That's great, but I'm in …
C: In trouble, yes! But there is a locker at JFK airport with a passport inside. Your photo's on it … and your new name … Olive Green.

Vocabulary

All right!	좋아요!	passport	여권
be in trouble	곤경에 빠지다	photo	사진
locker	물품 보관함	name	이름
airport	공항		

G: I'm not interested. I'm on vacation.

(…)

C: Ms Aguilar? You're not on vacation. You're in your flat in 9 Greenwood Avenue, Brooklyn. And you're in trouble.

G: Am I really?

C: Oh yes! Kirsch, your boss, is in prison … because of you.

G: He's in prison because he's a murderer.

C: Well … but it is your fault and his men are after you! The USA is a very dangerous place for you these days. But there is a way out!

G: What way out?

C: There is a locker at JFK Airport with a passport inside. Your photo is on it. And your new name … Olive Green.

G: All right! Enough! What's the job?

Vocabulary			
not	~이 아닌, ~하지 않는	be after	~을 쫓다, 찾다
interested	관심 있는	dangerous	위험한
be on vacation (AmE) / holiday (BrE)	휴가 중이다	place	곳, 장소
		these days	요즘에
flat	아파트	way out	해결책, 탈출구
be in trouble	곤경에 빠지다	locker	물품 보관함
really	정말로, 실제로	airport	공항
prison	감옥, 교도소	passport	여권
because of	~ 때문에	photo	사진
murderer	살인자, 살인범	name	이름
fault	탓, 잘못	All right!	알았어요!
man	부하, 아랫사람	Enough!	그만해요!

level A1 Scene 1

Grammar explanations

주격 인칭대명사

단수	복수
I	we
you	you
he/she	they
it	

be동사

단수

+

I am (I'm) a thief.
저는 도둑입니다.

You are (You're) a student.
당신은 학생입니다.

It is (It's) a dog.
그것은 개입니다.

−

I'm not a thief.
저는 도둑이 아닙니다.

You aren't a student.
당신은 학생이 아닙니다.

It isn't a dog.
그것은 개가 아닙니다.

?

Am I an art thief?
제가 도둑인가요?

Are you a student?
당신은 학생인가요?

Is it a dog?
그것은 개인가요?

+ / − (축약형)

Yes, I am.
네, 그래요.

No, I'm not.
아니요, 그렇지 않아요.

Yes, you are.
네, 그래요.

No, you aren't.
아니요, 그렇지 않아요.

Yes, it is.
네, 그래요.

No, it isn't.
아니요, 그렇지 않아요.

복수

+

We are (We're) students.
우리는 학생입니다.

You are (You're) art collectors.
당신들은 컨설턴트입니다.

They are (They're) consultants.
그들은 컨설턴트입니다.

−

We aren't students.
우리는 학생이 아닙니다.

You aren't art collectors.
당신들은 미술품 수집가가 아닙니다.

They aren't consultants.
그들은 컨설턴트가 아닙니다.

?

Are we students?
우리는 학생인가요?

Are you art collectors?
당신들은 미술품 수집가인가요?

Are they consultants?
그들은 컨설턴트인가요?

+ / − (축약형)

Yes, we are.
네, 그래요.

No, we aren't.
아니요, 그렇지 않아요.

Yes, you are.
네, 그래요.

No, you aren't.
아니요, 그렇지 않아요.

Yes, they are.
네, 그래요.

No, they aren't.
아니요, 그렇지 않아요.

소유격 인칭대명사

I	→ **my**	It's **my** phone. 그것은 제 전화기입니다.
you	→ **your**	What's **your** name? 당신의 이름은 무엇인가요?
he	→ **his**	**His** nationality is British. 그의 국적은 영국입니다.
she	→ **her**	**Her** boss is Dieter Kirsch. 그녀의 보스는 Dieter Kirsch입니다.
it	→ **its**	It's a nice phone. I like **its** colour. 멋진 전화기네요. 그것의 색깔이 마음에 들어요.
we	→ **our**	**Our** passports are in the locker. 우리의 여권은 물품 보관함 안에 있어요.
you	→ **your**	**Your** jobs are interesting. 당신의 일은 흥미롭군요.
they	→ **their**	Olive is **their** new art consultant. Olive는 그들의 새로운 미술품 컨설턴트입니다.

관사

1. 단수 명사 앞

    I am **a** student. 나는 학생입니다. (1명)
    cf. We are ~~a/an~~ students. 우리는 학생입니다. (2명 이상)

    You are **a** mechanic. 당신은 정비사입니다. (1명)
    cf. They are ~~a/an~~ mechanics. 그들은 정비사입니다. (2명 이상)

2. 「형용사 + 명사」 앞

    She is **a** talented thief. 그녀는 유능한 절도범입니다.
    He is **a** good partner. 그는 좋은 파트너입니다.
    cf. We are ~~a/an~~ young art consultants. 우리는 젊은 미술품 컨설턴트입니다.
      They are ~~a/an~~ interesting clients. 그들은 흥미로운 고객입니다.

3. 모음 발음 앞에는 **an**을 사용

    It's **an** interesting job offer. 흥미로운 일거리군요.
    I'm **an** artist. 저는 예술가입니다.

> **Remember!**
> It's **an** umbrella.
> cf. It's **a** university.
>
> She's **a** consultant.
> cf. She's **an** art consultant.

Communication situations

Read the following dialogues. Olive, Peter and James have just met at a language course.

Hello, my name is Olive Green. What's your name?

Dialogue 1

Peter: Hello, my name is Peter.
Olive: How are you today?
Peter: I'm fine, thanks. And you?
Olive: I'm fine. Thank you. Where are you from?
Peter: I'm from India.
Olive: So you are from Asia. And I'm sure you have got a mobile. What's your mobile number?
Peter: It's 03 03 88 56.
Olive: Could you repeat, please?
Peter: No problem. It's 03 03 88 56.
Olive: OK, now I got it right. Thanks.

Hello. 안녕하세요. | **What's your name?** 당신의 이름은 무엇인가요? | **How are you?** 오늘 기분이 어떠세요? | **Where are you from?** 어디에서 오셨어요? | **sure** 확신하는 | **mobile** 휴대폰 | **(phone) number** (전화) 번호 | **Could you repeat, please?** 다시 한번 말씀해 주시겠어요? | **Now I got it right.** 이제 제대로 알아들었어요.

Dialogue 2

James: Hi, I'm James.
Olive: Nice to meet you. Where are you from?
James: I come from Europe.
Olive: Oh, Europeans are always interesting to me. I'm American. And you? Are you German or French?
James: No, I am Polish.
Olive: And what do you do there?
James: I'm a teacher.
Olive: So, you work at school. Can I visit you?
James: Yes, you can. No problem.
Olive: What's your email address?
James: My email is: E-V-E-@-Y-A-H-O-O.C-O-M.
Olive: Thank you. Speak soon.

Hi. 안녕하세요. | **Nice to meet you.** 만나서 반가워요. | **come from** ~에서 오다, ~ 출신이다 | **What do you do?** 어떤 일을 하세요? | **teacher** 교사, 선생님 | **work at** ~에서 일하다 | **Speak soon.** 곧 연락해요.

Dialogue 3

Peter: Hello, my name is Peter.
Olive: How are you today?
Peter: I'm pretty well. And you?
Olive: Fine, thanks. Where do you come from?
Peter: I come from California.
Olive: Seriously? Me too!
Peter: That's very interesting!
Olive: And what's your job?
Peter: I'm a doctor.
Olive: What's your address?
Peter: I live on North Road 5.

I'm pretty well. 꽤 좋아요. | **Fine, thanks.** 좋아요, 고마워요. | **Seriously?** 정말이에요? | **Me too!** 저도 마찬가지예요! | **What's your job?** 무슨 일 하세요?

level A1 Scene 1

Vocabulary plus

course	강의, 강좌	See you soon!	곧 봐요!
good idea	좋은 생각	sick	아픈
It was nice talking to you!	대화 즐거웠어요!	sound	~처럼 들리다
Lucky you!	운이 좋으시네요!	Thanks for the chat.	이야기 나누어 줘서 고마워요.
ready	준비된	That's lovely.	멋지네요.
responsible	책임이 막중한; 책임이 있는	welcome to	~에 오신 것을 환영해요.
same	같은	when	~할 때
Say that again, please.	다시 한 번 말씀해 주세요.		

Cultural tips

Did you know that ...?

John F. Kennedy International Airport (JFK for short) is a major international airport located in New York, United States. It is the busiest international airport for people travelling to the United States. Over ninety airlines operate out of the airport to all 6 continents. It was opened in 1948 and renamed in 1963 in memory of John F. Kennedy, the 35th President of the United States, after his assassination.

Brooklyn is one of the 5 boroughs of New York City. It is located on the west end of Long Island.

UK is an abbreviation for the United Kingdom, and U.S. is an abbreviation for the United States.

The photo shows Manhattan and the Brooklyn Bridge viewed from Brooklyn.

Scene 2 — Film dialogue and vocabulary

Read the client's monologue. Check the list of words and phrases below.

That is the town of Old Berry. A nice, small town. Nothing special, really.

Those are the stone circles near the town. Officially, they are your work.

… because Olive Green is now a student of archaeology from the USA.

This is Campbell Manor. It's got 22 bedrooms, a big library and a park.

This is Robert Murray. Age: 55. Job: businessman. A clever and dangerous man.

That is Robert Murray's son, Curtis. Age: 28. He hasn't got a job, but he's got two important hobbies: drinking and women.

That is Beatrice Murray, maiden name: Campbell. She is Curtis's mother and the wife of Robert Murray. Age: 46. She's a housewife. Her hobby is gardening.

These paintings are the famous Murray collection.

And this is "Thistle Flowers". It's an impressionist masterpiece. These days it's worth 25, maybe 30 million pounds … Your job is to steal this painting for me.

level A1

Vocabulary

town	마을	important	중요한, 소중한
old	오래된	hobby	취미
nice	예쁜, 멋진, 좋은	drinking	음주
small	작은	woman	여자
nothing	아무것도	maiden name	(여성의) 결혼하기 전 성
special	특별한	mother	어머니, 엄마
stone	돌	wife	아내, 부인
circle	원, 동그라미	housewife	주부
near	~ 주변에	gardening	정원 가꾸기, 원예
officially	대외적으로는, 표면상으로는	painting	그림
work	과제, 연구, 일	famous	유명한
student	학생	collection	수집품, 소장품
archaeology	고고학	thistle	엉겅퀴
manor	저택	flower	꽃
bedroom	침실	impressionist	인상파의; 인상파 화가
big	커다란, 큰	masterpiece	걸작
library	서재; 도서관	worth	~의 가치가 있는
park	정원; 공원	maybe	어쩌면, 아마
businessman	사업가	million	100만
clever	영악한, 똑똑한	pound (pound sterling, GBP)	파운드 (영국의 화폐 단위)
son	아들	steal	훔치다
have (got)	가지고 있다		

Grammar explanations

지시 대명사 this, these, that, those

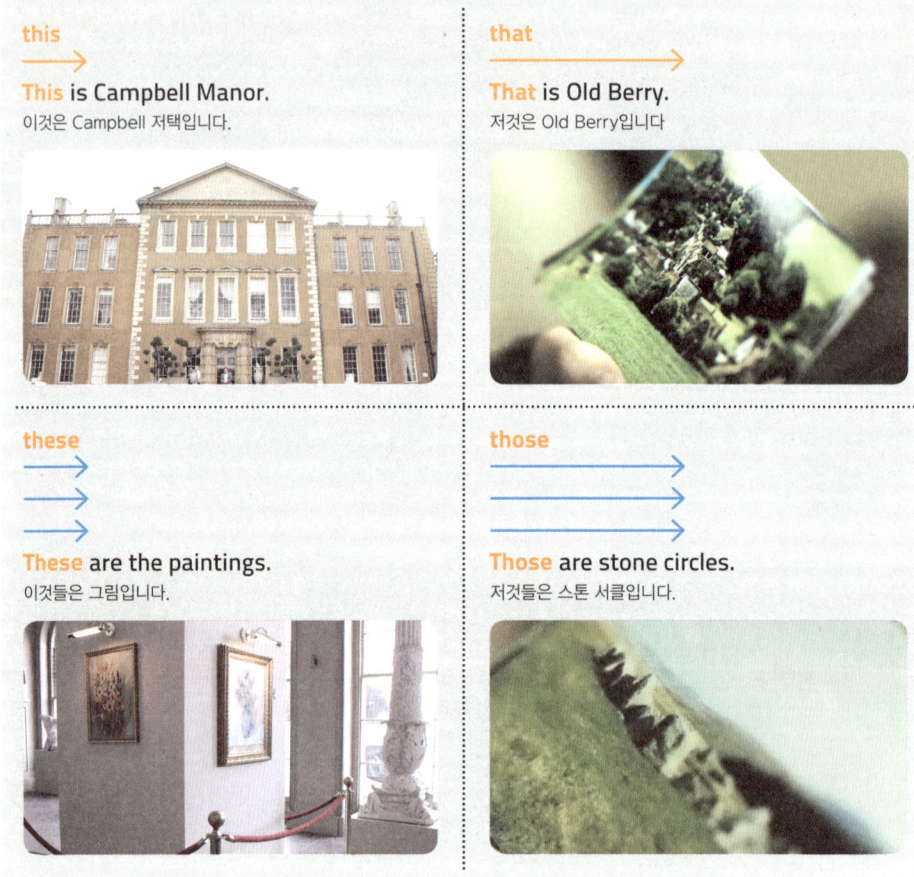

this
→
This is Campbell Manor.
이것은 Campbell 저택입니다.

that
→
That is Old Berry.
저것은 Old Berry입니다

these
→→→
These are the paintings.
이것들은 그림입니다.

those
→→→
Those are stone circles.
저것들은 스톤 서클입니다.

have got

+

I **have got** (I**'ve got**) a secret.
제게는 비밀이 있어요.

You **have got** (You**'ve got**) a BMW car.
당신은 BMW 자동차를 가지고 있어요.

He **has got** (He**'s got**) a famous painting.
그는 유명한 그림을 가지고 있어요.

She **has got** (She**'s got**) a garden.
그녀는 정원을 가지고 있어요.

It **has got** (It**'s got**) 22 bedrooms.
그곳에는 침실 22칸이 있어요.

We **have got** (We**'ve got**) an art collection.
우리는 미술품 컬렉션을 가지고 있어요.

You **have got** (You**'ve got**) a nice house.
당신들은 멋진 집을 가지고 있어요.

They **have got** (They**'ve got**) many rooms in their manor.
그들의 저택에는 많은 방이 있어요.

?

I **have got** a passport in the locker. ➔ **Have** I **got** a passport in the locker? 물품 보관함에 여권이 있나요?

Have you **got** a famous painting? 당신은 유명한 그림을 가지고 있나요?

Has he **got** two hobbies: women and drinking? 그가 여자와 음주라는 두 가지 취미를 가지고 있나요?

Has she **got** beautiful flowers in her garden? 그녀의 정원에 아름다운 꽃이 있나요?

Has it **got** 22 bedrooms? 그곳에 침실 22칸이 있나요?

We **have got** a nice flat. ➔ **Have** we **got** a nice flat? 우리에게 멋진 아파트가 있나요?

Have you **got** many visitors in Old Berry? Old Berry에 많은 방문객들이 오나요?

Have they **got** an impressionist masterpiece? 그들이 인상주의 걸작을 가지고 있나요?

명사의 소유격

Robert is Beatrice**'s** husband and Curtis**'s** father.

Beatrice is Robert**'s** wife and Curtis**'s** mother.

Curtis is Beatrice and Robert**'s** son.

➔ 단수 명사 + **'s**

What is Olive**'s** job? Olive의 직업은 무엇인가요?

This is Jessica**'s** house. 이곳은 Jessica의 집입니다.

➔ 복수 명사 + **'**

These are my sons**'** passports. 이것들은 내 아들들의 여권입니다.

➔ 두 개의 명사 + **'s**

Curtis is Beatrice and Robert**'s** son. Curtis는 Beatrice와 Robert의 아들입니다.

Campbell Manor is Beatrice and Robert**'s** family home. Campbell 저택은 Beatrice와 Robert의 집입니다.

Communication situations

Read the following dialogues between two people who want to know each other better.

Do you have a family?

Dialogue 1

B: Yes, I do.
A: Have you got any brothers or sisters?
B: Yes, I have got a brother and a sister.
A: Where do they live?
B: My brother lives in the UK.
A: And what about your sister?
B: My sister lives in Canada.

Have you got any brothers or sisters? 형제나 자매 있어요? I **brother** 오빠, 형, 남동생 I **sister** 언니, 누나, 여동생 I **Where?** 어디에요?

Dialogue 2

B: Well, it is difficult.
A: What do you mean? Are your parents gone?
B: No, they aren't, but we don't have a good relationship.
A: I see. And do you have any siblings?
B: No, I haven't. But I have a lot of friends.

---

well 음, 글쎄요 ㅣ **difficult** 곤란한, 어려운 ㅣ **What do you mean?** 무슨 뜻이죠? ㅣ **Are your parents gone?** 부모님께서 돌아가셨나요? ㅣ **I see.** 그렇군요. ㅣ **siblings** 형제자매 ㅣ **a lot of friends** 많은 친구

Dialogue 3

B: I don't want to talk about it.
A: Oh, come on. Just a few words, all right? So, do you have a family?
B: Yes, I do.
A: Have you got any brothers or sisters?
B: Yes, I have got a brother.
A: Where does he live?
B: My brother lives with my parents.

I don't want to talk about it. 그 이야기는 하고 싶지 않아요. ㅣ **Come on.** 그러지 말고요. ㅣ **Just a few words.** 몇 마디라도 해 보세요.

Dialogue 4

B: Well, it is difficult.
A: What do you mean? Are your parents gone?
B: My mother and father are dead.
A: And your parents' brothers or sisters?
B: My mother's brother lives in New York.
A: What does he do?
B: My uncle is an art consultant.

---

father 아버지, 아빠 | **be dead** 죽다

aunt	고모, 이모, 숙모	warm	마음이 따뜻한
emotional	감정적인, 정에 약한	What is she like?	그녀는 어떤 사람인가요?
mum	엄마		

Cultural tips

Did you know that …?

Road traffic in the United Kingdom is left-hand. This means that traffic keeps to the left side of the road. Other left-hand traffic countries include, for example: Ireland, Australia, South Africa, India, Kenya and New Zealand.

The photo shows the left-hand road traffic in central London.

Scene 3 — Film dialogue and vocabulary

Read the dialogue between Jessica (J), Olive (O) and David (D). Check the list of words and phrases below.

Good morning, luv. Sorry, that thing is broken!

A1-03-01

O: Good morning. My name's Olive Green. I have a room booked here.

J: Yes, yes, I have your reservation right here. You're here until next Friday, aren't you? Oh, sorry, silly me – I'm Jessica. I run the place. (…)

O: Yes?

J: Nothing. Are you single?

O: Excuse me?

J: Are you single?

D: Don't mind my mother. She wants to find a wife for me. Hi, I'm David. Nice to meet you.

O: I'm Olive. Nice to meet you, too.

J: David, be a good boy and take Ms Green's luggage to her room.

D: Boy, it's heavy! What have you got inside? Weapons and explosives? (…) Just kidding.

level **A1**

> Okay, let's go. It's room 5.

Vocabulary

Good morning.	안녕하세요.	Excuse me?	뭐라고요?
luv	당신, 자네, 자기	mind	신경 쓰다
Sorry!	미안해요!	want	원하다, 바라다
thing	것, 물건	find	찾아주다
broken	고장 난	Hi.	안녕하세요.
room	방, 객실	meet	만나다
booked	예약된	too	또한, 역시
here	이곳에, 여기에	be	되다
reservation	예약	boy	남자아이, 소년; 아들
until	~까지	take	가져다주다, 운반하다
next	다음	luggage	짐
Friday	금요일	heavy	무거운
silly	바보 같은, 어리석은	weapon	무기
Silly me!	내 정신 좀 봐!	explosive	폭발물
run	운영하다, 관리하다	Just kidding.	농담이에요.
single	결혼을 안 한; 애인이 없는	go	가다

level **A1** Scene 3

Grammar explanations

현재 시제

➜ 습관, 반복적인 일

Olive robs art collectors.
Olive는 미술품 수집가들을 텁니다.

Tourists visit Jessica's place (a B&B) every summer.
여름마다 관광객들이 Jessica의 숙소(B&B)를 찾습니다.

➜ 사실

Water boils at 100℃.
물은 섭씨 100도에서 끓습니다.

The Earth goes round the Sun.
지구는 태양 주위를 돕니다.

It snows in winter in the Alps.
겨울에는 알프스 산맥에 눈이 내립니다.

현재 시제와 어울리는 시간 표현

- **always**
- **every day, every week**
- **often**
- **usually**
- **sometimes**
- **seldom**
- **never**

3인칭 단수(he/she/it)의 현재형

1. k, n, l 등의 자음, e, 「모음 + y」로 끝나는 동사 ➜ **s**

   예) work ➜ **works**   run ➜ **runs**   take ➜ **takes**   enjoy ➜ **enjoys**

2. z, ch, sh, x, o로 끝나는 동사 ➜ **es**

   예) watch ➜ **watches**   finish ➜ **finishes**   do ➜ **does**

3. 「자음 + y」로 끝나는 동사 ➜ **ies**

   예) study ➜ **studies**   cry ➜ **cries**

현재 시제의 부정문

I run the place.
➜ I **do not (don't)** run the place. 저는 이곳을 운영하지 않습니다.

David listens to his mum.
➜ David **does not (doesn't)** listen to his mother. David는 엄마 말을 듣지 않습니다.

Olive does exercises.
➜ Olive **does not (doesn't)** do exercises. Olive는 운동을 하지 않습니다.

It takes 3 minutes.
➜ It **does not (doesn't)** take 3 minutes. 3분이 걸리지 않습니다.

We go to room 5.
➜ We **do not (don't)** go to room 5. 우리는 5호실로 가지 않습니다.

Communication situations

Read the following dialogues between a receptionist and a hotel guest.

Good morning and welcome to the Grand Hotel. How may I help you?

Dialogue 1

Guest: Hello, I have a room booked at your hotel.
Receptionist: What's your name, please?
Guest: I'm Sarah Jones.
Receptionist: One moment, please. Oh yes, Ms Jones. Welcome to our hotel. Here is your key.
Guest: Thank you.
Receptionist: Is there anything else I can do for you?
Guest: Yes. Do you have any sport facilities?
Receptionist: Yes, we do. There is a swimming pool, a sauna and a gym.
Guest: What time are they open?
Receptionist: All facilities are open from 9 a.m. till 9:30 p.m.
Guest: What time is the restaurant open?
Receptionist: We serve breakfast from 6:30 to 10. Lunch is from 12:00 to 4 p.m. and then the restaurant is open till 10:30 p.m.
Guest: OK. Thanks for your help.
Receptionist: My pleasure.

How may I help you? 무엇을 도와드릴까요? I **One moment.** 잠시만 기다려 주십시오. I **sport facilities** 운동 시설 I **gym** 체육관 I **from … to …** ~부터 ~까지 I **a.m.** 오전 I **p.m.** 오후 I **serve breakfast** 아침 식사를 제공하다 I **My pleasure.** 천만에요.

Dialogue 2

Guest: Good morning. I'd like to book a room, please.

Receptionist: Would you like a single or a double room?

Guest: I'd like to book a single room, please.

Receptionist: When would you like to check in?

Guest: On Tuesday morning.

Receptionist: What time, please?

Guest: I'd like to check in around 10:30 a.m.

Receptionist: OK. Thank you. How long would you like to stay?

Guest: Only one night.

Receptionist: And how would you like to pay: by credit card or cash?

Guest: I don't know yet.

Receptionist: OK, don't worry. You can decide later.

---

check in 체크인하다 | **on Tuesday morning** 화요일 오전에 | **What time?** 몇 시에 하시겠습니까? | **How long?** (기간이) 얼마나 | **pay** 결제하다, 내다 | **By credit card or by cash?** 신용 카드로 하시겠습니까, 현금으로 하시겠습니까? | **Don't worry.** 괜찮습니다., 걱정하지 마십시오. | **decide later** 나중에 결정하다

Dialogue 3

Guest: Hello, I'd like to change my booking.

Receptionist: Of course, no problem. May I have your name, please?

Guest: The booking is for Mr and Mrs Smith.

Receptionist: Your booking starts on Wednesday, the 3rd of May, and the checkout is on Friday, the 5th of May. What would you like to change?

Guest: I'd like to check in on Thursday.

Receptionist: Right. Let me confirm that: check-in on Thursday, the 4th of May and checkout on the 5th of May. Is that correct?

Guest: Yes, that's perfect. Thank you.

Receptionist: Is there anything else I can do for you?

Guest: No, that's all. Thank you.

May I have your name? 성함을 말씀해 주시겠습니까? | **checkout** 체크아웃 | **confirm** 확인하다 | **Is that correct?** 맞습니까? | **perfect** 완벽한 | **That's all.** 그게 다예요.

level A1 Scene 3

Vocabulary plus

Anything else?	더 필요한 것 있으십니까?
Anytime.	언제든지요.
A single or a double room?	싱글룸으로 하시겠습니까, 더블룸으로 하시겠습니까?
ask the chef to one's table	주방장을 테이블로 부르다
at midnight	자정에
at night	밤에
call the bellboy	벨보이를 부르다
closed	문을 닫은
Could I order some food?	음식 좀 주문할 수 있을까요?
Could you be more specific?	좀 더 구체적으로 말씀해 주시겠습니까?
Enjoy your stay!	계시는 동안 즐거운 시간 보내십시오!
Goodbye.	안녕히 가세요.
I beg your pardon?	뭐라고 말씀하셨죠?
I'm afraid not.	죄송하지만 안 됩니다.
in the late evening	저녁 늦게
in the meantime	그 사이에, 그 동안에
Just a second.	잠시만 기다려 주세요.
look forward to	~을 기대하다
make changes	바꾸다, 변경하다
on Monday afternoon	월요일 오후에
on the second floor	2층에
prepare	준비하다
reception desk	접수처, 프런트
something to eat	먹을 것
take a lift	엘리베이터를 타다
take the stairs	계단을 이용하다
Thank you for your help.	도와주셔서 감사합니다.
That's very kind of you.	정말 친절하시네요.
till Saturday	토요일까지
wake-up call	모닝콜
You are welcome.	천만에요.

Cultural tips

Did you know that ...?

There is not one correct way to say "hello" in English – it depends on the person you are greeting. To greet friends and family, you can use informal expressions like "Hello" or "Hi". With people you don't know so well, it is best to use more formal greetings. Say "Good morning" / "Good afternoon" and ask "How are you?" to find out if they are well. In most English-speaking countries, shaking hands is the most common greeting. Some people greet close friends with a hug or kiss on one or two cheeks (between men and women).

Scene 4

Film dialogue and vocabulary

Read the dialogue between Jessica (J) and Olive (O). Check the list of words and phrases below.

O: I'm fine, really. I'm not hungry.

J: Yes, you are. Don't be silly, darling. There is some homemade soup on the table.

O: For me?

Here you are, Olive! Please change and come for supper.

Vocabulary

please	부디, 제발
change	옷을 갈아입다
come	오다
supper	저녁 식사
fine	괜찮은
hungry	배고픈
darling	얘야
some	약간의
homemade	직접 만든, 집에서 만든
soup	수프
table	테이블, 탁자

A1-04-01

Read the dialogue between Jessica (J), Olive (O) and David (D). Check the list of words and phrases below.

Come and sit here, Olive.

Thank you. Wow, this looks amazing.

A1-04-02

34 Olive Green

level **A1**

J: Thank you. Tuck in! (…)

J: Okay children, it's time for me to go to bed, but you two stay here and enjoy the wine.

D: More wine?

O: Wine is a tricky thing. But then again … Why not?

D: So, tell me: why are you so interested in those old stones? They don't do anything! They're not even pretty. Your job seems awfully boring.

O: Why do you work as a policeman in Old Berry? How many criminals have you got in this town? Two?

D: You're so wrong! I solve many difficult cases every day.

O: Stolen bicycles? Drunk driving? Lost cats?

D: Lost cats are a serious matter. Think of the children that lose them.

O: I'm so sorry. Yes, you do a great job for the community.

Vocabulary			
sit	앉다	How many?	몇 개나요?
children	아이들	criminal	범죄자
time	시각	be wrong (about)	(~에 대해) 잘못 알고 있다
bed	침대	solve	해결하다, 풀다
stay	그대로 남다, 계속 있다	many	많은
enjoy	(술이나 음식을) 들다	difficult	어려운
wine	와인, 포도주	case	사건
tricky	묘한, 어려운	every day	날마다, 매일
But then again …	그래도…	stolen	도둑맞은
Why not?	좋죠!	bicycle	자전거
tell	말해주다	drunk driving	음주운전
anything	아무것도	lost	잃어버린, 행방불명된
even	~도, ~조차	cat	고양이
pretty	예쁜	serious	중대한, 심각한
seem	~인 것 같다	matter	문제
awfully	몹시	lose	잃어버리다
boring	지루한, 재미없는	community	지역 사회
policeman	경찰관		

Grammar explanations

현재 시제의 의문문

➜ 일반 동사 (go, take, fly, drive, drink, want, steal 등)

I **like** red wine. And you? **Do** you like red wine? 저는 레드 와인이 좋아요. 당신은요? 레드 와인을 좋아하나요?

Olive **stops** her car. Where **does** she stop it? Olive가 차를 세웁니다. 그녀는 어디에 차를 세우나요?

Beatrice **works** in the garden. **Does** she always work in the garden? Beatrice는 정원에서 일을 합니다. 그녀는 늘 정원에서 일하나요?

Where **do** they **live**? **Do** they live in Old Berry? Yes, David and Jessica **live** in Old Berry. 그들은 어디에 사나요? Old Berry에 사나요? 네, David와 Jessica는 Old Berry에 살아요.

➜ be동사

This **is** Robert Murray. **Is** he a businessman? Yes, he **is**. 이 사람은 Robert Murray예요. 그는 사업가인가요? 네, 그래요.

Are you a student of archaeology? No, I**'m** not. I **am** a student of history. 당신은 고고학과 학생인가요? 아니요, 그렇지 않아요. 저는 역사학과 학생이에요.

➜ have got

Have you **got** a flat in Old Berry? No, I **haven't**. I**'ve got** a room in a B&B. Old Berry에 당신 아파트가 있나요? 아니요, 그렇지 않아요. 저는 B&B에서 방을 얻었어요.

Has Curtis **got** a job? No, he **hasn't**. But he**'s got** two hobbies … Curtis는 직업이 있나요? 아니요, 그렇지 않아요. 하지만 두 개의 취미가 있는데…

대답

➜ yes

Do you steal paintings? Yes, I **do**. 당신은 그림을 훔치나요? 네, 그래요.

Does he do a great job for the community? Yes, he **does**. 그가 지역 사회를 위해 훌륭한 일을 하나요? 네, 그래요.

Do they work for Robert? Yes, they **do**. 그들은 Robert 밑에서 일하나요? 네, 그래요.

➜ no

Do I rob art collectors? No, I **do not** (I **don't**). 제가 미술품 수집가들을 터나요? 아니요, 그렇지 않아요.

Does she like the old stones? No, she **does not** (she **doesn't**). 그녀는 오래된 돌을 좋아하나요? 아니요, 그렇지 않아요.

Do we visit Old Berry? No, we **do not** (we **don't**). 우리는 Old Berry를 방문하나요? 아니요, 그렇지 않아요.

현재 시제와 어울리는 시간 표현

David **always** eats with his mum. David는 항상 엄마와 식사를 합니다.
Robert **often** does business with dangerous men. Robert는 위험한 사람들과 자주 거래합니다.
We **usually** drive to work. 우리는 보통 차로 출근합니다.
Olive **sometimes** tells the truth. Olive는 가끔 진실을 말합니다.
The Murrays **seldom** sit in the library. Murray 가족은 서재에 앉아 있을 때가 드뭅니다.
David **never** goes to the gym. David는 결코 체육관에 가지 않습니다.

I solve many cases **every day**. Curtis visits pubs **ever day**.
저는 매일 많은 사건을 해결합니다. Curtis는 매일 술집에 갑니다.

Olive does different exercises **every week**. She jogs, she swims, rides a horse and does kickboxing. There is a community meeting **every week**.
Olive는 매주 다른 운동을 합니다. 조깅, 수영, 승마, 그리고 킥복싱을 합니다. 매주 지역 사회 모임이 있습니다.

Olive steals one painting **every month**. Jessica has guests **every month**.
Olive는 매달 그림 한 점을 훔칩니다. Jessica는 매달 손님을 받습니다.

Olive changes country **every year**. Many tourists come to Old Berry **every year** to see the stone circles. Olive는 매년 다른 나라에 갑니다. 많은 관광객들이 해마다 스톤 서클을 보기 위해 Old Berry를 방문합니다.

Olive is in trouble **from time to time**. David plays snooker **from time to time**.
Olive는 이따금 곤경에 빠집니다. David는 이따금 스누커를 칩니다.

선호의 의미를 나타내는 표현

→ **like** (+ 동사 + -ing)
  I like driv**ing**. 저는 운전을 좋아합니다.
  He likes collect**ing** paintings.
  그는 미술품 수집을 좋아합니다.

→ **love** (+ 동사 + -ing)
  We love work**ing**. 우리는 일을 매우 좋아합니다.
  She loves jogg**ing**. 그녀는 조깅을 정말 좋아합니다.

→ **enjoy** (+ 동사 + -ing)
  You enjoy steal**ing**. 당신은 도둑질을 즐깁니다.
  It enjoys play**ing**. 그것은 놀이를 즐깁니다.

→ **be interested in** (+ 동사 + -ing)
  He is interested in do**ing** business.
  그는 사업하는 것에 관심이 있습니다.
  We are interested in tak**ing** photos.
  우리는 사진 찍는 것에 관심이 있습니다.

동명사

→ 자음 + 모음 + 자음 = 자음 반복 + **-ing**
  run → run**n**ing   swim → swim**m**ing

→ e로 끝나는 동사 = e + **-ing**
  tak**e** → tak**ing**   driv**e** → driv**ing**

→ y로 끝나는 동사 = y + **-ing**
  stud**y** → stud**y**ing   pla**y** → pla**y**ing

Communication situations

Read the following dialogues between Olive and David talking in the kitchen about food.

Hi, I'm glad you are home. I'm starving. Is there something to eat?

Dialogue 1

David: Mum always leaves lunch for us in the microwave.

Olive: Sure, sure, but I'm so hungry I have to eat something right now.

David: There is spaghetti in the fridge.

Olive: Can you put it in the microwave for me? I'll just wash my hands.

David: There is also some chicken rice.

Olive: No, thanks. I prefer spaghetti.

I'm glad you are home. 집에 계셔서 다행이에요. | **I'm starving.** 배고파 죽겠어요. | **have to** ~해야 한다 | **fridge** 냉장고 | **put ... in the microwave** ~을 전자레인지에 넣다

Dialogue 2

David: No, there isn't and I'm hungry too.

Olive: And Jessica is still at her Women's Institute meeting. Well, we have to prepare something. What would you like?

David: I want pancakes. Can you make them?

Olive: With your help, yes. Let's find some dishes.

David: Look at the sink. Everything is dirty.

Olive: Oops … Somebody has to wash it.

David: I hate washing up.

Olive: Stop moaning and get to work.

David: Where is the dish soap?

Olive: It's probably next to the sink, as always. Check before you ask.

---

meeting 모임, 회의 ׀ **pancake** 팬케이크 ׀ **look at** ~을 보다 ׀ **dirty** 더러운 ׀ **stop moaning** 불평을 멈추다 ׀ **get to work** 일을 시작하다 ׀ **dish soap** 주방 세제 ׀ **next to the sink** 싱크대 옆에

Dialogue 3

David: There are some sandwiches and a chicken salad.

Olive: Let's have the salad and take the sandwiches out.

David: Out? What for?

Olive: Today is Tuesday, so we go to the swimming pool. Don't you remember?

David: Oh, right … So, do you really want to start this diving course?

Olive: Yes, of course. And you don't?

David: No, I prefer swimming.

Olive: Well, at least give it a try. If you don't like it then you can just go back to swimming.

I prefer swimming. 저는 수영이 더 좋아요. ׀ **At least give it a try.** 그래도 시도는 해 보세요. ׀ **go back to** ~으로 돌아가다

Vocabulary plus

A pot or a saucepan?	그냥 냄비요, 아니면 스튜 냄비요?
bake an apple pie	사과 파이를 굽다
behind the kettle	주전자 뒤에
big fan of water sports	수상 스포츠를 매우 좋아하는 사람
both	둘 다
broken	깨진; 고장 난
can cook	요리할 수 있다
Come on!	그러지 말고요!
dish towel	(접시 닦는) 행주
dishwasher	식기세척기
frying pan	프라이팬
give	주다
give something up	~을 포기하다, 그만두다
glass	유리잔
go shopping	장을 보다
Guess!	맞춰 보세요!
handball championship	핸드볼 선수권 대회
Here you are.	여기 있어요.
Hurry up!	서둘러요!
I feel sick.	몸이 안 좋아요.
I like basketball.	저는 농구를 좋아해요.
I love football.	저는 축구를 좋아해요.
I want to dry my hands.	손의 물기를 닦고 싶어요.
It hangs somewhere.	어딘가에 걸려 있어요.
It's your turn.	당신 차례예요.
I've got a headache.	두통이 있어요.
know the answer	답을 알다
lay the table	상을 차리다
look around	주위를 둘러보다
lose to	~에게 지다
near the oven	오븐 주위에
noisy	시끄러운
paper towels	페이퍼 타올
pour	따르다, 붓다
surprise	뜻밖의 선물; 놀라운 소식
take out	~을 꺼내다
tickets for a match	운동 경기 티켓
That's not true.	그렇지 않아요.
The counter is wet.	조리대에 물기가 있어요.
washing-up liquid	주방용 세제
You can do it!	당신은 할 수 있어요!

Cultural tips

Did you know that ...?

When you sit at the table and are about to start eating, you can use a couple of nice phrases to begin the meal: "Enjoy your meal", "Have a good lunch", or simply "Enjoy". In the UK, with friends and family, you can use an informal phrase: "Tuck in".

Scene 5   Film dialogue and vocabulary

Read the dialogue between David (D) and Olive (O). Check the list of words and phrases below.

Hi! Care for some company?

You're a jogger then?

D: Yeah, sort of. As a police officer, I need to stay fit.
O: All right, show me what you've got. (...)
O: Are you okay? Do you need a break?
D: I'm okay ... but maybe some water.
O: It's not such a bad town.
D: Come on, it's lovely! And there's everything here: pubs, a community centre, a swimming pool, even a small cinema ...
O: Does it do 3D? You know, we Americans only watch 3D movies.
D: No, it doesn't. But there are interesting things to do and even some business opportunities, too ... And some nice people ... There are many nice people in Old Berry.
O: Yeah, I know a few of them.
D: Look, I know you're only in the town for a short time, but ... Would you like to go out for a drink with me?

Vocabulary			
care for	~을 원하다; ~을 좋아하다	community centre	지역 센터
company	친구, 동료	swimming pool	수영장
jogger	조깅하는 사람	cinema	극장, 영화관
Sort of.	그런 셈이죠.	watch	보다, 관람하다
as	~으로서	movie (AmE) / film (BrE)	영화
police officer	경찰관	interesting	재미있는, 흥미로운
need to	~해야 한다	opportunity	기회
fit	건강한, 탄탄한	people	사람들
show	보여 주다	know	알다
break	휴식	a few	몇의, 약간의
water	물	Look.	저기요., 있잖아요.
such	그렇게	short	(시간이) 짧은
bad	나쁜	would like to	~하고 싶다
lovely	멋진, 매력적인	go out	외출하다, 나가다
everything	모든 것	go out for a drink	한잔하러 가다
pub	술집, 선술집		

What should Olive do?

O: David, it's not a good idea. I need to finish my project.
D: But I know everything about local history! Going out with me is good for your project!
O: Is it? ... All right then! ... Are you ready for some more jogging?

Vocabulary		
	idea	생각
	finish	끝내다, 마치다
	project	프로젝트, 과제
	local	지역의, 현지의
	history	역사
	about	~에 대한
	ready (for)	(~할) 준비된
	jogging	조깅

O: The answer is 'yes', but only because I like your mum and want to see her happy.
D: Great! That's so kind of you.
O: "Kind" is my middle name. Are you ready for some more jogging?

Vocabulary					
	answer	대답		kind	상냥한, 친절한
	only	순전히, 단지		middle name	가운데 이름
	mum	엄마		ready (for)	(~할) 준비가 된
	see	보다		jogging	조깅
	happy	기쁜, 행복한			

Grammar explanations

there is/are

	there **is** ... (단수)	there **are** ... (복수)
+	**There is (There's)** a swimming pool in Old Berry. Old Berry에는 수영장이 있습니다. **There is (There's)** a small cinema in Old Berry. Old Berry에는 작은 극장이 있습니다. **There is (There's)** a bench in the park. 공원에는 벤치가 있습니다.	**There are (There're)** pubs in Old Berry. Old Berry에는 술집들이 있습니다. **There are (There're)** some business opportunities in Old Berry. Old Berry에는 사업 기회들이 있습니다. **There are (There're)** nice people in Old Berry. Old Berry에는 좋은 사람들이 있습니다.
?	**Is there** a swimming pool in Old Berry? Old Berry에 수영장이 있나요?	**Are there** pubs in Old Berry? Old Berry에 술집들이 있나요?
+/−	Yes, **there is**. 네, 있어요. No, **there is not (isn't)**. 아니요, 없어요.	Yes, **there are**. 네, 있어요. No, **there are not (aren't)**. 아니요, 없어요.

전치사

There is a sofa **on** the floor. 바닥에 소파가 있습니다.

There is a box **under** the window. 창문 아래에 상자가 있습니다.

There is a lamp **between** the red sofa and the window. 붉은색 소파와 창문 사이에 스탠드가 있습니다.
There is one door **in** the room. 방 안에 문이 하나 있습니다.
There is a flower **next** to the mirror. 거울 옆에 꽃이 있습니다.
The curtains are **behind** the chest. 커튼은 서랍장 뒤에 있습니다.
Olive is **in front of** the window. Olive는 창문 앞에 있습니다.

관사

a/an

➜ 처음 말하는 것일 때 (모음 발음 앞에는 an을 사용)

It's **an** old town. 그것은 오래된 마을입니다.
He's **a** new client. 그는 새로운 고객입니다.

the

➜ 전에 언급했던 것을 말할 때

It's not **a** bad town. – Come on, **the** town is lovely. 나쁜 동네는 아니네요. – 왜 그래요, 멋진 곳이잖아요.
Where is **the** airport in Old Berry? Old Berry의 공항은 어디에 있나요? (Old Berry에 공항이 하나뿐일 때)

관사를 쓰지 않는 경우

➜ 복수 명사 앞

There are ~~(a/an/the)~~ pubs in Old Berry.
Old Berry에는 술집들이 있습니다.

➜ 국적 앞

We are ~~(a/an/the)~~ Americans and we watch only 3D movies. 우리는 미국인이라 3D 영화만을 봅니다.

➜ 도시명 및 국가명 앞

I live in ~~(a/an/the)~~ Old Berry. 저는 Old Berry에 삽니다.
She doesn't live in ~~(a/an/the)~~ London. She lives in ~~(a/an/the)~~ New York. 그녀는 런던에 살지 않습니다. 뉴욕에 삽니다.
Are you from ~~(a/an/the)~~ Poland? 당신은 폴란드 출신인가요?

Remember!

the UK
(the United Kingdom)

the USA
(the United States of America)

Communication situations

Read the following dialogues between Olive and David who are about to go on a date in Old Berry.

Hi David, I'm ready to go.

Dialogue 1

David: Great. Where would you like to go?
Olive: I'd like to see the nightlife in Old Berry.
David: All right. Let's hit the town!
Olive: Great! What's the plan?
David: First, a restaurant, then a pub or a romantic walk.
Olive: It sounds nice but not very dynamic. Do you have a plan B?
David: I want to show you the old town by night.
Olive: Oh, lovely! And then?
David: Would you like to watch a film?
Olive: Yeah, let's go to the movie theater.
David: Wait, I asked about a cinema not a theatre.
Olive: David, I'd love to watch a film. In New York we go to a "movie theater" and here, in the UK, you have a "cinema", right?

---

nightlife 밤 문화 | **hit the town** (시내에 가서) 재미있게 놀다 | **What's the plan?** 계획이 어떻게 되나요? | **romantic walk** 로맨틱한 산책 | **dynamic** 활동적인, 활동 있는 | **Do you have a plan B?** 2안도 있나요? | **old town** 오래된 마을 | **movie theater** 영화관 | **theatre** 극장

Dialogue 2

David: That's OK but my mum isn't ready yet.
Olive: Erm ... Is it a date with you and your mum?
David: Just kidding! So, what would you like to do?
Olive: I'd like to see the nightlife in Old Berry.
David: What exactly would you like to see?
Olive: Something I won't find in a tourist guide. Impress me.
David: Let me show you the railway station.
Olive: The railway station? What's so amazing about the railway station?
David: There is an ice rink and a disco there.
Olive: Fantastic! And what do we choose: the disco or ice skating?
David: Let's go to the disco.
Olive: Hmm, or maybe an hour of ice skating and then the disco? I love ice skating!
David: Sure, why not.

tourist guide 관광 안내 책자 | **Impress me.** 저를 감동시켜 보세요. | **railway station** 기차역 | **ice rink** 아이스 링크, 스케이트장 | **ice skating** 아이스 스케이트 타기

Dialogue 3

David: Perfect. Let's go catch a bus then.
Olive: Excuse me? A bus?
David: Well, yes. There is no underground in Old Berry.
Olive: Underground? Oh, you mean subway. OK, never mind. Don't you have a car?
David: I do but it is broken.
Olive: OK, OK, let's walk to the bus stop. How far is that?
David: By taxi 10 minutes, on foot more than 30.
Olive: I can't believe we have to take a taxi to get to the bus stop ...

catch a bus 버스를 타다 | **underground** (영) 지하철; (미) 지하도 | **subway** (미) 지하철 | **bus stop** 버스 정류장 | **How far is that?** 얼마나 걸리나요? | **on foot** 걸어서, 도보로 | **take a taxi** 택시를 타다

Vocabulary plus

an hour and a half	1시간 30분	Let me show you.	제가 보여 드릴게요., 제가 가르쳐 드릴게요.
band	밴드, 악단	Let's enjoy the evening.	저녁을 즐겁게 보냅시다.
bookstore	책방, 서점	local church	지역 교회
Bye!	잘 가요!	Maybe some other time.	다음에요.
concert hall	콘서트홀, 공연장		
department store	백화점	petrol	휘발유, 가솔린
Do you have a better idea?	더 좋은 생각 있어요?	place	자리, 장소, 집
Have fun!	즐거운 시간 보내세요!	post office	우체국
How long does it take to get to ...?	~까지 가는 데 얼마나 걸리나요?	red light	(신호등의) 빨간불
I can't wait!	정말 기대돼요!	shopping mall	쇼핑몰
If we miss the bus ...	만약 버스를 놓치면…	small town	소도시
Is there something wrong?	무슨 문제 있어요?	start blinking	깜빡이기 시작하다
It costs a lot.	돈이 많이 들어요.	tank the gasoline	휘발유를 채우다
It's going to be fun, I can feel it.	재미있을 거예요, 느낌이 와요.	waste time for	~에 시간을 낭비하다
		What's wrong with that?	그게 뭐 어때서요?

Cultural tips

Did you know that ...?

There are some differences between the English language used in the UK and U.S. David is English and he uses words like "cinema" and "film", whereas Olive is American and she uses words like "movie theater" and "movie", respectively. You can see more examples of the differences in the wordlist in this lesson.

level A1 Scene 5

Scene 6

Film dialogue and vocabulary

Read the dialogue between the barman, David (D) and Bill (B). Check the list of words and phrases below.

One more pint of lager and one more whiskey on the rocks!

D: Not the pool! I don't know how to impress you!

B: David, you are a lucky man! She's lovely!

D: Bill, weren't you in prison?

B: The prison you put me in!

D: What can I say, Bill ... You deserved it!

B: What's your name, lovely girl? She's not very talkative, that's a good thing! I adore women like that! You don't meet many of them these days!

D: Bill, that's enough!

level A1

Vocabulary				
one	하나	put	집어넣다
more	더	say	말하다
pint	파인트	What can I say?	어쩌겠어?
lager	라거	deserve	~을 받을 만하다
whiskey on the rocks	얼음 넣은 위스키	girl	아가씨, (젊은) 여자
pool	포켓볼	talkative	말이 많은, 수다스러운
impress	감동시키다	adore	아주 좋아하다, 흠모하다
lucky	운이 좋은		

Read the dialogue between Olive (O) and David (D). Check the list of words and phrases below.

This date was a bad idea.

A1-06-02

O: I really need to finish my project now. I have no time for …
D: A loser like me?
O: Good night, David.

date	데이트	Good night.	잘 자요., 잘 가요.
loser	못난 사람, 낙오자		

level A1 Scene 6   51

Grammar explanations

과거 시제

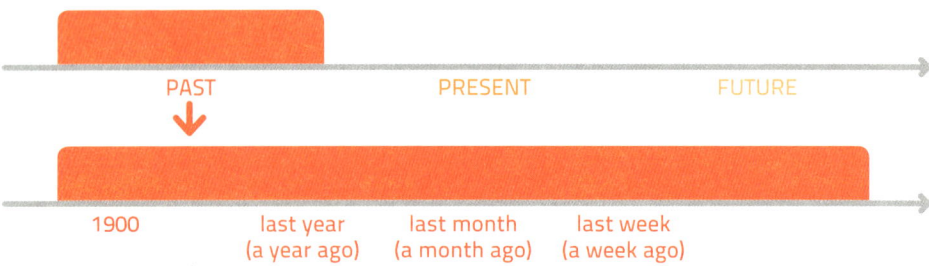

현재 시제	과거 시제
I **am** your student today. 저는 오늘 당신의 학생입니다.	I **was** your student yesterday. 저는 어제 당신의 학생이었습니다.
You **are** at home today. 당신은 오늘 집에 있습니다.	You **were** at home last weekend. 당신은 지난 주말에 집에 있었습니다.
Olive **is** in the UK these days. Olive는 요즘 영국에 있습니다.	Olive **was** in the USA last month. Olive는 지난달에 미국에 있었습니다.
Curtis **is** in a pub every Friday. Curtis는 금요일마다 술집에 갑니다.	Curtis **was** in a pub last Friday. Curtis는 지난 금요일에 술집에 갔습니다.
Oh, it **is** a beautiful summer this year. 오, 올해 여름은 아름답습니다.	Oh, it **was** a beautiful summer last year. 오, 작년 여름은 아름다웠습니다.
We **are** in this park every morning. 우리는 매일 아침 이 공원에 옵니다.	We **were** in this park yesterday morning. 우리는 어제 아침 이 공원에 왔습니다.
You **are** happy in Old Berry this summer. 당신들은 이번 여름에 Old Berry에서 행복합니다.	You **were** happy in Old Berry last summer. 당신들은 작년 여름 Old Berry에서 행복했습니다.
They **are** in their park now. 그들은 지금 정원에 있습니다.	They **were** in their park 3 days ago. 그들은 3일 전에 정원에 있었습니다.

규칙 동사의 과거형

finish → finish**ed**   watch → watch**ed**   need → need**ed**
call → call**ed**   talk → talk**ed**   want → want**ed**
solve → solv**ed** (e = -ed)

! enj**o**y → enjoy**ed** (모음 + y = -ed)
! st**a**y → stay**ed** (모음 + y = -ed)
! stud**y** → stud**ied** (모음 + 자음 + y = -ied)
! sto**p** → sto**pped** (자음 + 모음 = 자음 반복 + -ed)

불규칙 동사의 과거형

be	→ was/were	have	→ had	say	→ said
come	→ came	know	→ knew	see	→ saw
do	→ did	meet	→ met	steal	→ stole
drink	→ drank	put	→ put	take	→ took
eat	→ ate	run	→ ran	tell	→ told
go	→ went				

의문사

What?

What's your name? 이름이 무엇인가요?

What do you do in the evenings? – I always **watch** the news on TV.
저녁에는 무엇을 하나요? – 항상 TV로 뉴스를 봐요.

When?

When were you in New York? – I was there **last winter**. 언제 뉴욕에 있었나요? – 작년 겨울에 있었어요.

When does she usually jog in the park? – Olive usually jogs **in the mornings**.
그녀는 보통 언제 공원에서 조깅을 하나요? – Olive는 보통 아침에 조깅을 해요.

Where?

Where do you live? – I live **in London**. 어디에 사나요? – 런던에 살아요.

Where is your phone? – It's **in my bag**, I think.
당신 전화기는 어디에 있나요? – 제 가방 안에 있을 거예요.

Which?

Which car do you like: the blue or the red one? – I like the **blue car**.
파란색과 빨간색 자동차 중에 어떤 것이 마음에 드나요? – 파란색 차가 마음에 들어요.

Which books do you read: criminals or horrors? – **Horrors**, of course.
범죄 소설과 공포 소설 중에 어떤 책을 읽나요? – 당연히 공포 소설이죠.

cf. **What** cars do you like? – I like **Italian cars**.
　　 어떤 차를 좋아하나요? – 이탈리아 차를 좋아해요. (선택의 범위가 정해져 있지 않을 때)

would like

Would you **like to have** supper with us? – Yes. That's a lovely idea. Thank you.
저희와 같이 저녁 드실래요? – 네. 좋은 생각이군요. 고마워요.

Would you **like** something to eat? – Yes, please. Some soup, please.
먹을 것을 드릴까요? – 네, 부탁해요. 수프 주세요.

Would you **like** a cup of coffee? – No, thank you.
커피 한 잔 드실래요? – 고맙지만 사양할게요.

Would you **like** some wine? – Wine is a tricky thing … But yes, please.
와인 좀 드릴까요? – 와인은 묘한 술이죠… 그렇지만 네, 주세요.

Communication situations

Read the following dialogues in a restaurant.

Good evening Sir, how can I help you?

Dialogue 1

Client: I have a table booked here.

Waiter: Can I have your name, please?

Client: My name is John Smith.

Waiter: A moment please. Yes, Mr Smith. The table is waiting for you. Come with me, please. Can I take your order?

Client: What is the chef's speciality?

Waiter: It's tomato soup for the starter, steak with mashed potatoes and mixed salads for the main course and strawberries and cream for the dessert.

Client: I'll just have the main course, please.

Waiter: All right. May I offer you something to drink?

Client: Yes. A pint of lager, please.

Waiter: Of course, Sir. Thank you for the order. I'll be back with you shortly.

Good evening. 안녕하세요. | **table** 테이블 | **order** 주문 | **chef's speciality** 주방장 특선 요리 | **main course** 메인 요리 | **May I offer you ...?** ~을 드릴까요? | **I'll be back with you shortly.** 금방 가져다드리겠습니다.

Olive Green

Dialogue 2

Client: A table for two, please.
Waiter: Do you have a reservation?
Client: No, I don't.
Waiter: I'm afraid we don't have a table for you right now. Would you like to wait in the bar?
Client: Yes, I would.
Waiter: Follow me, please. Have a seat here. Can I get you something?
Client: A glass of white wine, please.
Waiter: Would you like it dry, semi-dry or sweet?
Client: Semi-dry, please. And can I get the bill for the wine?
Waiter: The wine will be on the bill with the restaurant order.
Client: Oh, perfect.
Waiter: Enjoy the wine!

Follow me, please. 저를 따라오십시오. | **glass** 잔 | **semi-dry** (와인이) 약간 드라이한

Dialogue 3

Client: A table for one, please.
Waiter: I'm afraid we don't have a table for you right now. Would you like to wait in the bar?
Client: No, thank you. Can I have any table then?
Waiter: I'm sorry but we are fully booked. Could you come back in an hour?
Client: OK. I'll come in an hour then.
Waiter: Would you like to make a booking?
Client: No, I'll just try my luck with you later.
Waiter: All right. See you later then.

We are fully booked. 예약이 꽉 찼습니다. | **in an hour** 한 시간 뒤에 | **make a booking** 예약을 하다

Vocabulary plus

a bottle of mineral water	생수 한 병	hot chocolate sauce	뜨거운 초콜릿 소스
Are you joking?	농담하시는 거예요?	red wine	레드 와인, 적포도주
Come this way, please.	이쪽으로 오십시오.	roast beef	로스트비프
cup	컵	soft drinks	(알코올 성분이 없는) 음료
green peas	청완두	sparkling water	탄산수
Have a nice day!	좋은 하루 보내십시오!	vegetarian meals	채식 요리

Cultural tips

Did you know that ...?

A **pub**, or public house, is a house licensed to sell alcoholic drinks to the general public in the UK, Ireland, New Zealand, Canada, and Australia. In many places, especially in villages, a pub is the central point for the local community. Most pubs offer beers, wines, spirits, soft drinks and snacks.

A **pint** is a unit of volume of about 0.568 litres.

Lager is a type of beer that is conditioned at low temperatures.

Whiskey on the rocks means that you will be served whiskey over ice. "Rocks" basically means "ice".

Scene 7
Film dialogue and vocabulary

Read the dialogue between Curtis (C), Olive (O) and Murray (M). Check the list of words and phrases below.

C: My father doesn't let anyone in! You need to know a special code to enter the door.
O: But you're such a smart boy and you know the code.
M: Who's your friend, Curtis?
C: Dad, I thought you went to London yesterday.
M: I didn't. Robert Murray, but please call me Robert.
O: I'm Olive Green. Nice to meet you Mr Mur ... Robert.
M: So Curtis, you wanted to show your guest my paintings. All right, why don't we see them together? (...)

level A1

It's mum. I need to ... er ...

M: You go and talk to her, son. Let me entertain your guest for a minute. "Thistle Flowers" ... The best work of Frederic Beaumont. Some people think he was the most talented of the Impressionists. Did you know that when he painted it in 1880 ...

O: 1879. I study archeology. This stuff interests me.

M: Olive, you're very different from all Curtis's other girlfriends. Most of them pretend to be classy and smart, but you pretend to be vulgar and stupid. Why do you do that?

Vocabulary				
	dad	아빠	minute	잠깐; (시간 단위) 분
	precious	진귀한	best	최고의, 가장 훌륭한
	father	아버지	the Impressionists	인상파 화가들
	code	비밀번호	when	~할 때
	enter	들어가다	paint	그리다
	door	문	study	공부하다
	smart	똑똑한	stuff	것
	friend	친구	interest	관심을 끌다
	yesterday	어제	different (from)	(~와) 다르다
	call	부르다	girlfriend	(여자) 애인, 여자 친구
	guest	손님	pretend	~인 척하다
	together	다 같이, 함께	classy	우아한
	talk (to)	(~와) 말하다, 통화하다	vulgar	저속한, 천박한
	entertain	접대하다	stupid	멍청한

level A1 Scene 7

What should Olive do?

flirt with Murray

show surprise

O: Maybe I'm not here for Curtis.

M: Well, then … In that case, my clever American friend …

C: I'm sorry, Olive, there's something I need to deal with. Let me give you a lift back into town, okay?

O: Yes, sure.

O: I have no idea what you're talking about!

M: But I think you do, Ms Green!

C: I'm sorry, Olive, there's something I need to deal with. Let me give you a lift into town, okay?

O: Yes, sure.

M: It's Murray. I need information about a girl. She's American. Her name's Olive Green …

Vocabulary		
	in that case	그런 경우라면, 그렇다면
	something	어떤 일
	deal with	~을 처리하다
	give a lift	태워주다

Vocabulary		
	something	어떤 일
	deal with	~을 처리하다
	give a lift	태워주다
	information	정보

Grammar explanations

be동사의 과거형

단수

I **was** in that house last month.
저는 지난달에 저 집에 있었어요.

Was I in that house last month?
제가 지난달에 저 집에 있었나요?

Yes, I **was**. / No, I **was not** (I **wasn't**).
네, 그랬어요. / 아니요, 그렇지 않았어요.

David, you **were** with Olive yesterday.
David, 당신은 어제 Olive와 함께 있었어요.

David, **were** you with Olive yesterday?
David, 당신은 어제 Olive와 함께 있었나요?

You, you **were**. / No, you **were not** (you **weren't**).
네, 그랬어요. / 아니요, 그렇지 않았어요.

Olive **was** with Robert in his gallery.
Olive는 Robert와 함께 화랑에 있었어요.

Was Olive with Robert in his gallery?
Olive가 Robert와 함께 화랑에 있었나요?

Yes, she **was**. / No, she **was not** (she **wasn't**). 네, 그랬어요. / 아니요, 그렇지 않았어요.

Curtis **was** in the room too.
Curtis도 방에 있었어요.

Was Curtis in the room too?
Curtis도 방에 있었나요?

Yes, he **was**. / No, he **was not** (he **wasn't**). 네, 그랬어요. / 아니요, 그렇지 않았어요.

It **was** a precious painting.
그것은 귀중한 그림이었어요.

Was it a precious painting?
그것이 귀중한 그림이었나요?

Yes, it **was**. / No, it **was not** (it **wasn't**).
네, 그랬어요. / 아니요, 그렇지 않았어요.

복수

We **were** in Jessica's B&B last summer.
우리는 지난 여름 Jessica의 B&B에 묵었어요.

Were we in Jessica's B&B last summer?
우리가 지난 여름 Jessica의 B&B에 묵었나요?

Yes, we **were**. / No, we **were not** (we **weren't**). 네, 그랬어요. / 아니요, 그렇지 않았어요.

You **were** with Olive and David in the pub. 당신들은 Olive와 David와 함께 술집에 있었어요.

Were you with Olive and David in the pub?
당신들은 Olive와 David와 함께 술집에 있었나요?

Yes, you **were**. / No, you **were not** (you **weren't**). 네, 그랬어요. / 아니요, 그렇지 않았어요.

Olive and Curtis **were** in Robert's room.
Olive와 Curtis는 Robert의 방에 있었어요.

Were Olive and Curtis in Robert's room?
Olive와 Curtis가 Robert의 방에 있었나요?

Yes, they **were**. / No, they **were not** (they **weren't**).
네, 그랬어요. / 아니요, 그렇지 않았어요.

Grammar explanations

과거 시제의 의문문과 대답

단수

I **started** a Polish course 3 weeks ago.
저는 3주 전에 폴란드어 수업을 시작했어요.

Did I **start** a Polish course 3 weeks ago?
제가 3주 전에 폴란드어 수업을 시작했나요?

Yes, I **did**. / No, I **did not** (I **didn't**).
네, 그랬어요. / 아니요, 그렇지 않았어요.

You **made** a delicious supper.
맛있는 저녁을 만들었군요.

Did you **make** a delicious supper?
맛있는 저녁을 만들었나요?

Yes, you **did**. / No, you **did not** (you **didn't**).
네, 그랬어요. / 아니요, 그렇지 않았어요.

Curtis **drove** the car. Curtis가 차를 몰았어요.

Did Curtis **drive** the car?
Curtis가 차를 몰았나요?

Yes, he **did**. / No, he **did not** (he **didn't**).
네, 그랬어요. / 아니요, 그렇지 않았어요.

Olive **came** to Old Berry to see the stone circles.
Olive는 스톤 서클을 보기 위해 Old Berry에 왔어요.

Did Olive **come** to Old Berry to see the stone circles?
Olive가 스톤 서클을 보기 위해 Old Berry에 왔나요?

Yes, she **did**. / No, she **did not** (she **didn't**). 네, 그랬어요. / 아니요, 그렇지 않았어요.

The painting **looked** amazing.
그 그림은 굉장해 보였어요.

Did the painting **look** amazing?
그 그림이 굉장해 보였나요?

Yes, it **did**. / No, it **did not** (it **didn't**).
네, 그랬어요. / 아니요, 그렇지 않았어요.

복수

We **watched** all the scenes of Olive Green. 우리는 Olive Green의 모든 장면을 보았어요.

Did we **watch** all the scenes of Olive Green? 우리가 Olive Green의 모든 장면을 보았나요?

Yes, we **did**. / No, we **did not** (we **didn't**). 네, 그랬어요. / 아니요, 그렇지 않았어요.

You **saw** the precious painting in Robert's room.
당신들은 Robert의 방에서 귀중한 그림을 보았어요.

Did you **see** the precious painting in Robert's room?
당신들은 Robert의 방에서 귀중한 그림을 보았나요?

Yes, you **did**. / No, you **did not** (you **didn't**). 네, 그랬어요. / 아니요, 그렇지 않았어요.

Olive and Curtis **left** Campbell Manor together.
Olive와 Curtis는 함께 Campbell 저택을 떠났어요.

Did they **leave** Campbell Manor together?
그들이 함께 Campbell 저택을 떠났나요?

Yes, they **did**. / No, they **did not** (they **didn't**). 네, 그랬어요. / 아니요, 그렇지 않았어요.

과거 시제의 부정문

I **did not visit** Campbell Manor. (I **didn't**) 저는 Campbell 저택을 방문하지 않았습니다.
You **did not visit** Old Berry. (you **didn't**) 당신은 Old Berry를 방문하지 않았습니다.
Olive **did not talk** to Beatrice. (she **didn't**) Olive는 Beatrice와 대화하지 않았습니다.
David **did not have** a girlfriend. (he **didn't**) David에게는 여자 친구가 없었습니다.
The phone **did not work**. (it **didn't**) 그 전화기는 작동하지 않았습니다.
We **did not stay** at Jessica's place. (we **didn't**) 우리는 Jessica의 숙소에 머무르지 않았습니다.
You **did not take** photos of the stone circles. (you **didn't**) 당신들은 스톤 서클의 사진을 찍지 않았습니다.
Olive and Curtis **did not run** in the park together. (they **didn't**) Olive와 Curtis는 공원에서 함께 달리지 않았습니다.

형용사의 비교급

➜ 1음절인 경우 ➜ + **-er**
    old ➜ old**er**
    small ➜ small**er**

➜ 2음절이고 y로 끝나는 경우 ➜ + **-ier**
    funn**y** ➜ funn**ier**
    prett**y** ➜ prett**ier**

➜ 「자음 + 모음 + 자음」으로 이루어진 경우
    ➜ 자음 반복 + **-er**
    hot ➜ ho**tt**er
    big ➜ bi**gg**er
    sad ➜ sa**dd**er

➜ 2음절 이상인 경우 ➜ **more** + 형용사
    boring ➜ **more** boring
    important ➜ **more** important

Remember!

good ➜ **better** : He is a good businessman but Robert is a better one. 그는 수완 좋은 사업가이지만 Robert가 더 수완이 좋은 사업가입니다.

bad ➜ **worse** : Today the weather is bad but yesterday it was worse. 오늘도 날씨가 안 좋지만 어제 날씨는 더 좋지 않았습니다.

A than B
A is bi**gger than** B and B is small**er than** A. A는 B보다 크고 B는 A보다 작다.

Communication situations

Read the following dialogues between Olive and Murray about Campbell Manor.

Mr Murray ... Erm ... Robert! Thank you for showing me around. Your house is a real old mansion of English aristocracy.

Dialogue 1

Murray: That's true. It comes from the 19th century.

Olive: Is it true that there are 25 bedrooms, a chapel, a dining room and a ballroom here?

Murray: Don't forget about the library.

Olive: A library! I love such places. Could I see it?

Murray: Of course. This way.

Olive: Wow! It's enormous. And there are some paintings, too. Is this your famous gallery?

Murray: No. My gallery is much bigger and more valuable than that ...

Olive: It must be really impressive then. I would love to see it, Robert.

Murray: I don't show it to everyone but your smile is so charming ...

Olive: I'm really honoured. There are legends about your gallery, you know.

Murray: What legends?

Olive: Well, people say that you steal the masterpieces for your collection.

Murray: They are jealous.

Olive: Yes, I'm sure they are.

Thank you for showing me around. 구경시켜 주셔서 감사해요. | old mansion 오래된 저택 | 19th century 19세기 | dining room 식당 | valuable 진귀한, 가치 있는 | I'd like to see it. 무척 보고 싶어요. | Your smile is so charming. 미소가 정말 아름다우시네요. | honoured 영광스러운 | jealous 질투 나는

Dialogue 2

Murray: Well, my great-grandfather built it in the 19th century.

Olive: Wait a minute. It's called Campbell Manor, not Murray Manor.

Murray: Smart girl. You got me there.

Olive: So what's the true story, Robert?

Murray: My relative built it and Beatrice's bought it.

Olive: Robert, you are just pulling my leg now! But never mind. What's your favourite place here?

Murray: My garage.

Olive: Is it because of the Bentley collection?

Murray: Yes. The oldest car is from 1920.

Olive: That's quite impressive. Can we go for a ride?

great-grandfather 증조부 | Wait a minute. 잠깐만요. | You got me there. 제가 한 방 먹었네요. | true story 진짜 이야기, 속사정 | You are just pull my leg! 저를 놀리시는 거군요! | Never mind. 괜찮아요.. 신경 쓰지 마세요. | go for a ride (자동차 등을) 타러 가다

Dialogue 3

Murray: Come this way.

Olive: And that door? Where does it lead to?

Murray: To my office.

Olive: Could I see it?

Murray: No!

Olive: Hmm, I'm intrigued by your quick answer. I wonder what you hide in there.

lead to (문 등이) ~로 통하다 | I'm intrigued by ~에 호기심이 생기네요 | quick answer 다급한 대답

level A1 Scene 7

Vocabulary plus

ancestors	선조들, 조상들
arch	아치형 장식, 아치형 구조물
art gallery	화랑, 미술관
assume	추정하다
ban on hunting	사냥 금지
blacksmith	대장장이
cellar	지하 저장고
cleaning service	청소 서비스
count	세다
different story	다른 이야기
Don't you think?	그렇게 생각하지 않나요?
fascinating man	매력적인 남자
first female lawyer	최초의 여성 변호사
founder of the family	가문을 만든 사람
get into dancing	춤에 흥미를 붙이다, 춤에 맛 들다
grandmother	할머니
guest house	손님 숙소
have a lisp	혀 짧은 소리를 내다
hunting room	헌팅룸 (사냥 도구나 전리품을 전시해 놓은 방)
I'll be happy to show it to you.	기꺼이 보여줄게요.
I'm not that interested.	별로 관심 없어요.
in the pink dress	분홍색 드레스를 입고
keep the rest	나머지를 보관하다
Let's skip it.	그건 건너뜁시다.
lose one's mind	정신을 놓다
maintain	유지하다
noble face	귀한 인상, 고상한 얼굴
Oh dear.	이것 참., 맙소사.
originally	원래
outsource	외부에 위탁하다
playroom	아이들 놀이방
poor	가난한
real scum	완전 쓰레기 같은 놈
safe	안전한; 금고
secret place	비밀 장소
sensitive to beauty	아름다움을 민감하게 느끼는
servant house	하인들이 묵는 숙소
small part	일부
That's no reason to ...	그렇다고 ~할 이유는 없죠.
That's quite unusual for their times.	당시로서는 흔치 않은 일이네요.
The acoustic there is marvellous.	그곳의 음향시설은 훌륭해요.
thick	두꺼운
very much respected	매우 존경받는
We are on the same page.	다 이해했습니다.
Where the hell is ...?	대체 ~이 어디에 있죠?
You never know with people.	사람 일은 모르는 거예요.

Cultural tips

Did you know that …?

In English, there are some titles used before a person's name: "Mr" for men regardless of their marital status, "Mrs" for married women, "Ms" for women regardless of their marital status, "Miss" for girls and young women who are usually unmarried. For example, Mr David Owen, Mrs Jessica Owen, Ms Olive Green. First names are used in less formal situations, among friends etc. and when someone asks you to use their first name.

Scene 8

Film dialogue and vocabulary

Read Olive's monologue. Check the list of words and phrases below.

The fence ... that's easy.

A1-08-01

I can cut through it. I can climb over it, but the cameras …
Perhaps I can hack the cameras, but no … That's too risky!
There's a stream flowing across the Campbell estate. There are no cameras there.
I can swim along it but …
Nope! I'm no James Bond, for Christ's sake!
How can I enter the building without anyone seeing me? And more importantly …
How can I leave the building and escape without anyone seeing me?

Vocabulary

fence	울타리, 담장		stream	냇물, 개울
easy	쉬운		flow	흐르다
cut through	(날카로운 도구를 이용해) 뚫고 들어가다		estate	사유지, 부지
			swim	헤엄치다, 수영하다
climb	기어오르다		For Christ's sake!	젠장!
camera	카메라		building	건물
perhaps	아마		without	~하지 않고, ~ 없이
hack	해킹하다		more importantly	더 중요한 것은
too	너무, 지나치게		leave	벗어나다, 떠나다
risky	위험한		escape	달아나다, 탈출하다

Olive Green

Read the dialogue between Olive (O) and Curtis (C). Check the list of words and phrases below.

C: I'm glad you're still awake. Look, tomorrow in the evening there is a big charity party at the Manor. A very boring event, with lots of boring people coming.

O: Poor you, I'm very sorry to hear that!

C: Would you like to go with me? You can … make this thing more fun for me.

O: Sure! I'd love to come.

Vocabulary

glad	다행인, 기쁜
be awake	깨어 있다
still	아직, 여전히
tomorrow	내일
party	파티, 모임
charity party	자선 파티
event	행사
lots of	많은
Poor you!	불쌍하네요!, 안됐네요!
hear	듣다
make	만들다
fun	재미있는
Sure!	좋아요!

Grammar explanations

can/can't

단수

Can I hack the camera? 내가 카메라를 해킹할 수 있을까?
No, I **can't**. That's too risky. 아니, 못 해. 그건 너무 위험해.

Can you make this party more fun? 당신이 이번 파티를 더 재미있게 해 줄 수 있나요?
Yes, I **can**. And I'd love to go with you, Curtis. 네, 그럴 수 있죠. 그리고 당신과 함께 가고 싶어요, Curtis.

Can Curtis do anything to help Olive? Curtis가 Olive를 돕기 위해 무언가를 할 수 있을까요?
Yes, he **can**. He **can** invite her to the party. 네, 할 수 있어요. 그녀를 파티에 초대할 수 있죠.

Can she swim along the stream? 그녀가 냇물을 따라 헤엄칠 수 있을까요?
No, she **can't**. She is not James Bond. 아니요, 못해요. 그녀는 제임스 본드가 아니니까요.

Can a camera at Campbell Manor see Olive? Campbell 저택의 카메라가 Olive를 볼 수 있을까요?
Yes, it **can**. Of course it **can**. 네, 볼 수 있어요. 당연히 볼 수 있죠.

복수

Can we see some paintings? 우리가 그림을 볼 수 있을까요?
No, we **can't**. Only my father can open this door.
아니요, 그럴 수 없어요. 아버지만 이 문을 열 수 있어요.

Can you watch the film with me? 저와 함께 영화를 볼 수 있나요?
Yes, we **can**. We **can** entertain together. 네, 볼 수 있죠. 같이 즐길 수 있어요.

Can they call me today with all the information about Olive?
그들이 오늘 제게 전화해서 Olive에 관한 정보를 모두 알려 줄 수 있을까요?
No, they **can't**. They **can** call you tomorrow and give you what you need.
아니요, 그럴 수 없어요. 내일 전화해서 당신에게 필요한 것을 알려 줄 거에요.

+	I / you / he / she / it / we / you / they	can	동사 (do, see, go)
−		can't (cannot)	
?	Can	I / you / he / she / it / we / you / they	
+/−	Yes, No,		can. can't (cannot).

방향 및 이동의 의미를 나타내는 전치사

through – through the fence 울타리를 넘어서
over – over the wall 벽 위로
along – along the manor 저택을 따라서
up – up the stairs 계단 위로
down – down the stairs 계단 아래로
across – across the street 거리를 가로질러서
around – around the manor 저택 주위에
in – in the manor 저택 안에서
out – out of the manor 저택 밖으로

Communication situations

Read the following dialogues between two friends – Olive and Alfie.

Hello! How are you today? How is your day?

Dialogue 1

Alfie: Hi Olive. I'm fine, thanks, and you?

Olive: I'm OK, thank you. What are you up to these days?

Alfie: Well, I'm stuck at home.

Olive: What happened?

Alfie: Don't even ask.

Olive: Oh, come on. You can tell me. I won't laugh, I promise.

Alfie: I have broken my leg.

Olive: Your leg? How did that happen?

Alfie: I climbed up the ladder to hang the curtains and …

Olive: OK, OK, I don't want to know the rest! So I guess you are not coming to the concert tomorrow?

Alfie: No, no, I can go!

Olive: Can you? Really? With a broken leg? Oh, come on, don't be silly!

How is your day? 오늘 하루 어떻게 보내고 있어? | **What are you up to these days?** 요즘 어떻게 지내? | **I'm stuck at home.** 집에만 틀어박혀 있어. | **What happened?** 무슨 일 있어? | **Don't even ask.** 묻지도 마. | **I won't laugh, I promise.** 안 웃을게, 약속해. | **break** 부러뜨리다; 부러지다 | **climb up the ladder** 사다리에 오르다 | **hang the curtains** 커튼을 달다 | **Don't be silly!** 말도 안 되는 소리 하지 마!

Dialogue 2

Alfie: Hello! Hello? I can't hear you. Could you repeat, please?
Olive: Yes, hello, it's Olive here.
Alfie: Now I can hear you better. How are you?
Olive: I'm fine, thanks. I'm calling you because I have two tickets for a rock concert. Would you like to come?
Alfie: Are you joking? Of course I'd like to come!
Olive: The concert is on September 5th. It starts at 8 p.m.
Alfie: That's perfect. I'll pick you up at 6:45.
Olive: OK. See you at 6:45 then.

I can't hear you. 안 들려요. | **I'll pick you up at ...** 내가 ~시에 데리러 갈게

Dialogue 3

Alfie: Hi Olive, what's up?
Olive: Hi, I'm calling to ask about your plans for the weekend. Are you doing anything?
Alfie: Well, I'm seeing my family on Sunday but on Saturday I'm free.
Olive: All right. Hmm, I'm going jogging on Saturday morning. Would you like to join me?
Alfie: Have you lost your mind? I hate jogging.
Olive: OK, I understand. No problem. Maybe we'll meet up for something different some other time.

What's up? 무슨 일이야? | **I'm free.** 난 한가해. | **Would you like to join me?** 같이 갈래?

Dialogue 4

Alfie: I'm going to the cinema.
Olive: Sounds like a cool plan. Why don't we go together?
Alfie: Well, why not.
Olive: All right. I'll meet you at the cinema at 7:45.
Alfie: OK. Please buy the tickets if I'm late.
Olive: No problem, I will.

Vocabulary plus

a bit earlier	좀 더 일찍	I'm having a party.	파티를 열 거야.
as soon as possible	가능한 한 빨리	I'm sleeping.	나는 자고 있어.
at that time	그때	It's not my kind of music.	내가 좋아하는 종류의 음악이 아니야.
Christmas	크리스마스	next year	내년
fall from the ski lift	스키 리프트에서 떨어지다	See you there.	거기서 보죠.
Get well soon!	어서 나아!	shaken, not stirred	젓지 말고 흔들어서
go skiing	스키 타러 가다	Shall I bring something?	뭐 가져갈까?
I bet it hurt.	아팠겠다.	take place	열리다, 개최되다
I hope you can make it.	너도 와 줬으면 좋겠어.	unfortunately	안타깝게도
I'll be waiting for your call.	연락 기다릴게.	We'll catch up next time.	다음에 연락하자.
I'll do my best.	최선을 다할게.	What a pity!	안됐다!
I'll keep my fingers crossed!	행운을 빌게!	Why don't you come over?	놀러 올래?
I'll let you know.	알려 줄게.	Why don't you pop in?	잠깐 들를래?
I'll try.	한번 해 볼게.		

Cultural tips

Did you know that ...?

James Bond is a fictional British Secret Service agent created by writer Ian Fleming in his book in 1953. The character has also been adapted for TV, radio, comic strips, video games and films.

Scene 9

Film dialogue and vocabulary

Read the dialogue between Olive (O) and a shop assistant (S). Check the list of words and phrases below.

I'm looking for something fancy for a night out.

Does "a night out" mean going to the pub?

O: No, it means going to a formal dinner with the friends of the royal family.

S: Hm, I see ... Well then, this shop is the perfect place for you. We sell all kinds of evening dresses.

O: Oh, you do?

S: No, we don't. Women don't buy evening dresses in Old Berry. Sorry.

Vocabulary				
look for	~을 찾다	family	가족
fancy	멋진, 화려한	sell	팔다, 판매하다
mean	의미하다	kind	종류
formal	격식 차린	evening dress	이브닝드레스
dinner	만찬, 정찬	buy	사다, 구매하다
royal	왕실의		

What should Olive do?

insist — A1-09-02

leave — A1-09-03

O: For some reason, I don't believe you. Shall we look for something nice together? (…)

O: That looks … nice. Why didn't you tell me you had it?

S: Look, I'm trying to lose weight. Every day I look at this dress and I say to myself "I want to be slim enough to wear it!" But as you can see …

O: I'll take it.

S: Come back. I think I have something for you.

O: That looks … nice. Why didn't you tell me you had it?

S: Look, I'm trying to lose weight. Every day I look at this dress and I say to myself "I want to be slim enough to wear it!" But as you can see …

O: I'll take it.

Vocabulary

for some reason	왠지, 어떤 이유에서인지
believe	믿다, 신뢰하다
look	~하게 보인다
try to	~하려고 노력하다, 애쓰다
lose weight	살을 빼다
slim	날씬한
wear	입다

Vocabulary

come back	돌아오다
look	~하게 보인다
try to	~하려고 노력하다, 애쓰다
lose weight	살을 빼다
slim	날씬한
wear	입다

Grammar explanations

현재진행

→ 말하는 시점에 일어나고 있는 현재의 활동

Good morning, I'**m** look**ing** for a dress. 안녕하세요, 드레스를 찾고 있는데요.

It'**s** rain**ing** outside. Don't go out. 밖에 비가 오고 있어요. 나가지 마세요.

Olive, come and sit with us. We'**re** hav**ing** a lovely dinner. Olive, 와서 우리와 함께 앉아요. 근사한 저녁을 먹고 있어요.

→ 평소와 다른 현재의 활동

Robert's men usually don't work hard but they **are** work**ing** a lot **these days**. They **are** collect**ing** information about Olive. Robert의 부하들은 평소에 일을 열심히 하지 않지만, 요즘 많은 일을 하고 있습니다. 그들은 Olive에 관한 정보를 수집하고 있습니다.

Olive doesn't read a lot about archaeology but **now** in Old Berry she **is** read**ing** many books about the stone circles. Olive는 고고학에 관한 책을 많이 읽는 편은 아니지만, 현재 Old Berry에서 스톤 서클에 관한 책을 많이 읽고 있습니다.

→ 가까운 미래에 예정된 활동이나 행동

Olive **is** leav**ing** Old Berry next Friday. Olive는 다음 주 금요일에 Old Berry를 떠날 것입니다.

Curtis **is** see**ing** Olive tonight. Curtis는 오늘 밤 Olive를 만날 것입니다.

+

I **am** driv**ing** to Old Berry. Can I call you back?
제가 차를 몰고 Old Berry로 가고 있는 중이라서요. 제가 다시 전화해도 될까요?

You **are** try**ing** to understand Present Continuous.
당신은 현재진행을 이해하려고 노력하고 있습니다.

David **is** check**ing** Olive's laptop.
David는 Olive의 노트북을 확인하고 있습니다.

Olive **is** look**ing** at the maps of Campbell Manor.
Olive는 Campbell 저택의 지도를 보고 있습니다.

The phone **is** ring**ing**. Answer it!
전화기가 울리잖아요. 받으세요!

We **are** visit**ing** the stone circles in Old Berry.
우리는 Old Berry의 스톤 서클을 방문할 것입니다.

You **are** ask**ing** too many questions.
당신은 너무 많은 질문을 하고 있어요.

Olive and Curtis **are** go**ing** out together.
Olive와 Curtis가 데이트 중입니다.

−

I **am not** see**ing** my friend tonight.
저는 오늘 밤에 친구를 만나지 않을 거예요.

You **are not** study**ing** archeology in school now.
당신은 지금 학교에서 고고학을 공부하고 있지 않아요.

David is in Olive's room but he **is not** do**ing** the right thing.
David는 Olive의 방에 있는데 옳은 일을 하고 있지 않습니다.

The shop assistant **is not** help**ing** Olive.
매장 직원은 Olive를 돕고 있지 않습니다.

It **is not** rain**ing** outside. You can go out.
밖에 비가 오고 있지 않아요. 나가도 좋아요.

We **are not** hav**ing** a nice time in the pub.
우리는 술집에서 즐거운 시간을 보내고 있지 않습니다.

You **are not** read**ing** it for the first time.
당신은 그것을 처음 읽고 있는 것이 아니에요.

The cameras at Campbell Manor **are not** work**ing** at the moment.
Campbell 저택의 카메라들은 지금 작동하고 있지 않습니다.

Remember! 현재진행의 축약형

+

I **am** doing = I**'m** doing
you **are** doing = you**'re** doing
he **is** doing = he**'s** doing
we **are** doing = we**'re** doing
you **are** doing = you**'re** doing
they **are** doing = they**'re** doing

−

I **am not** doing = I**'m not** doing
you **are not** doing = you**'re not** doing = you **aren't** doing
he **is not** doing = he**'s not** doing = he **isn't** doing
we **are not** doing = we**'re not** doing = we **aren't** doing
you **are not** doing = you**'re not** doing = you **aren't** doing
they **are not** doing = they**'re not** doing = they **aren't** doing

현재진행의 의문문과 대답

단수

I **am** talk**ing** to you.
저는 당신에게 이야기하고 있어요.

Am I talk**ing** to you?
제가 당신에게 이야기하고 있나요?

Yes, I **am**. / No, I **am not** (I'**m not**).
네, 그래요. / 아니요, 그렇지 않아요.

You **are** do**ing** a great job for the community.
당신은 지역 사회를 위해 훌륭한 일을 하고 있어요.

Are you do**ing** a great job for the community?
당신은 지역 사회를 위해 훌륭한 일을 하고 있나요?

Yes, you **are**. No, you **are not** (you **aren't**).
네, 그래요. / 아니요, 그렇지 않아요.

He/She **is** mak**ing** progress in English.
그/그녀는 영어 실력이 늘고 있어요.

Is he/she mak**ing** progress in English?
그/그녀는 영어 실력이 늘고 있나요?

Yes, he/she **is**. / No, he/she **is not** (he/she **isn't**).
네, 그래요. / 아니요, 그렇지 않아요.

It **is** gett**ing** dark.
점점 어두워지고 있어요.

Is it gett**ing** dark?
점점 어두워지고 있나요?

Yes, it **is**. / No, it **is not** (it **isn't**).
네, 그래요. / 아니요, 그렇지 않아요.

복수

We **are** work**ing** hard.
우리는 열심히 일하고 있어요.

Are we work**ing** hard?
우리가 열심히 일하고 있나요?

Yes, we **are**. / No, we **are not** (we **aren't**).
네, 그래요. / 아니요, 그렇지 않아요.

You **are** leav**ing** next week.
당신들은 다음 주에 떠날 거예요.

Are you leav**ing** next week?
당신들은 다음 주에 떠날 건가요?

Yes, you **are**. / No, you **are not** (you **aren't**).
네, 그래요. / 아니요, 그렇지 않아요.

New guests **are** com**ing** in 3 or 4 days.
새로운 손님들은 3일이나 4일 후에 올 거예요.

Are new guests com**ing** in 3 or 4 days?
새로운 손님들은 3일이나 4일 후에 올 건가요?

Yes, they **are**. / No, they **are not** (they **aren't**).
네, 그래요. / 아니요, 그렇지 않아요.

She likes Old Berry. 그녀는 Old Berry를 좋아해요.
cf. She is liking Old Berry. (✗)

Beatrice loves gardening. Beatrice는 정원 가꾸기를 좋아해요.
cf. Beatrice is loving gardening. (✗)

Women hate vulgar men. 여자들은 무례한 남자를 싫어해요.
cf. Women are hating vulgar men. (✗)

I believe in you. 저는 당신을 믿어요.
cf. I am believing in you. (✗)

Remember!
like, love, hate, believe 등과 같은 동사는 현재진행형으로 쓰이지 않는다.

Communication situations

Read the following dialogues between a shop assistant and a client in a newsagent's, as well as a clothes and shoe shop.

Hello, can I help you?

Dialogue 1

Client: Yes, I'm looking for Harry Potter.

Shop assistant: But this is not a bookshop! It's a newsagent's. We sell newspapers, magazines, tissues, phone cards …

Client: Oh, I'm sorry.

Shop assistant: That's OK. I'll tell you where the bookshop is. Can you see the bakery?

Client: Yes, I can.

Shop assistant: The bookshop is opposite to the bakery.

Client: Oh yes, I can see it now.

Shop assistant: That's the ticket. Have a nice day!

Can I help you? 도와드릴까요? | **newsagent's** 신문 가판대 | **tissue** 티슈 | **bakery** 제과점, 빵집 | **opposite to** ~의 건너편에 | **I can see it now.** 이제야 보이네요. | **That's the ticket.** 바로 그거예요.

Olive Green

Dialogue 2

Client: Yes, I'm looking for something nice.

Shop assistant: Sure. Are you interested in shoes, trousers, shirts or dresses?

Client: I'd like to buy a new pair of shoes.

Shop assistant: The shoe department is on the second floor. Follow me please. What type of shoes are you looking for?

Client: I'd like to see some leather boots.

Shop assistant: Of course. In what colour?

Client: Black, please. And no shoelaces, only a zip.

Shop assistant: I'm sorry, but we don't have any shoes without shoelaces.

a new pair of shoes 새 신발 한 켤레 | **leather boots** 가죽 부츠 | **In what colour?** 무슨 색상으로요?

Dialogue 3

Client: Oh, yes. Have you got these jeans in a different colour?

Shop assistant: Sure. Would you like them in black or blue?

Client: Blue, please.

(...)

Shop assistant: Is everything fine with this pair?

Client: A 10 is too tight. I need a bigger size.

Shop assistant: Sure, here you are.

Client: Thanks. How much is it?

Shop assistant: It's £56. And the cash desk is over there.

in a different colour 다른 색으로 | **How much is it?** 얼마죠? | **cash desk** 계산대

Dialogue 4

Client: Yes, I'm looking for something nice.

Shop assistant: Sure. Are you interested in shoes, trousers, shirts or dresses?

Client: Trousers. Well, jeans, actually.

Shop assistant: No problem. What size are you? 10 or 12?

Client: I'm not sure.

Shop assistant: I'll bring you both. Here you are. The changing rooms are over there.

What size are you? 치수가 어떻게 되세요? | **changing rooms** 탈의실

Vocabulary plus

altogether	모두 합쳐, 총	Let me check.	확인해 보겠습니다.
a packet of tissues	티슈 한 묶음	Likewise.	마찬가지예요., 동감이에요.
between	~ 사이에, ~끼리	on the corner	모퉁이에
book department	서적 코너	reddish	불그스름한
casual	격식을 차리지 않는; 평상복	regular client	단골 손님, 고정 거래처
chemist	약국	smart shoes	세련된 신발
feel free	편하게 하다	Thanks for your help.	도와주셔서 고마워요.
fit	(옷 등이) 맞다	That'd be great.	그래 주면 좋지.
get a discount	할인받다	trainers	운동화
go with	~와 어울리다	try on	~을 입어보다, 신어보다
high heels	하이힐	two-year warranty	2년 품질 보증
I didn't catch that.	못 들었어요.		

Olive Green

Cultural tips

Did you know that ...?

The British Royal Family comprises the monarch (king or queen) of the United Kingdom and their close relations. Buckingham Palace is the London residence and headquarters of the reigning monarch of the United Kingdom.

The photo shows the Buckingham Palace in London.

Scene 10 — Film dialogue and vocabulary

Read the dialogue between Curtis (C), Olive (O) and Beatrice (B). Check the list of words and phrases below.

This is Olive. Olive, meet Beatrice.

Will you fetch your mum something to drink?

A1-10-01

B: You know, Olive, my son attracts two types of women. The first type of women are even more stupid than he is. He leaves them with broken hearts. The other type are smarter than Curtis and usually want to use him for our money. My … beloved husband is very good at making them go away! But you … My husband is interested in you. So, I guess, that makes you even smarter than he thinks you are. Olive, my husband will not make you happy. His money will not make you happy. I know that better than anyone.

Vocabulary

fetch	가지고 오다	money	돈
attract	(흥미를) 끌다	beloved	사랑하는
type	부류, 종류	husband	남편
first	첫 번째의	go away	떠나다
broken heart	(이별로 인한) 상심	guess	추측하다, 짐작하다
usually	보통, 대개	better	더 잘, 더 많이
use	이용하다		

level **A1**

Read the dialogue between Curtis (C) and Olive (O). Check the list of words and phrases below.

| Help! | 도와줘요!, 살려줘요! | give one's regards | 안부를 전하다 |

Grammar explanations

will

PAST NOW (PRESENT) FUTURE

All the guests **will notice** Olive at the party tomorrow. 내일 파티에서 모든 게스트들이 Olive를 주목할 것입니다.

Robert's money **will not make** Olive happy. Robert의 돈은 Olive를 행복하게 해 주지 못할 것입니다.

Will Olive's plan **work**? We **will see** soon. Olive의 계획이 성공할까요? 곧 알게 되겠죠.

Olive **will not be** in Old Berry next year. She **will be** in another country, somewhere in Europe. 내년에 Olive는 Old Berry에 있지 않을 것입니다. 유럽 어딘가의 다른 나라에 있을 것입니다.

will과 어울리는 전형적인 시간 표현:

in a few hours, tomorrow, next week/month/year, in 2075

단수

I'll (I **will**) see the stone circles one day.
저는 언젠가 스톤 서클을 볼 거예요.

You'll (you **will**) be just another girl for him, Olive.
당신은 그에게 그저 또 다른 여자가 될 거예요, Olive.

He/She'll (he/she **will**) do all the exercises correctly tonight.
그/그녀는 오늘 밤 모든 운동을 제대로 할 것입니다.

Olive's plan **will** (it'll) work perfectly next time.
다음에는 Olive의 계획이 완벽하게 성공할 것입니다.

복수

We'll (we **will**) visit Jessica's B&B in summer.
우리는 여름에 Jessica의 B&B를 방문할 거예요.

You'll (you **will**) sell out all the dresses in my shop very soon.
당신들은 곧 제 가게의 모든 드레스를 판매하게 될 거예요.

Olive and Curtis **will** (they'll) say hello to Beatrice at the party tonight.
Olive와 Curtis는 오늘 밤 파티에서 Beatrice에게 인사할 것입니다.

will이 들어간 부정문

+

Robert **will observe** Olive the whole evening.
Robert는 저녁 내내 Olive를 관찰할 것입니다.

Beatrice **will observe** Robert.
Beatrice는 Robert를 관찰할 것입니다.

Curtis **will be** with Olive and Olive ...
Curtis는 Olive와 함께 있을 것이고 Olive는…

Olive **will make** Curtis fall asleep.
Olive는 Curtis를 잠들게 만들 것입니다.

−

David **will not go** to the party. He doesn't have an invitation.
David는 파티에 가지 않을 것입니다. 초대장이 없습니다.

Olive **won't listen** to Beatrice's words at the party in the evening. Olive는 저녁 파티에서 Beatrice의 말을 귀담아듣지 않을 것입니다.

Robert **will not talk** to Olive.
Robert는 Olive와 이야기하지 않을 것입니다.

The bodyguards **won't help** David.
경호원들은 David를 돕지 않을 것입니다.

will이 들어간 의문문과 대답

+

Will my plan **work**? Yes, **it will**.
제 계획이 성공할까요? 네, 그럴 거예요.

Will you **drive** me home? Yes, **I will**.
저를 차로 집까지 데려다 줄 건가요? 네, 그럴 거예요.

Will they **jog** again? Yes, **they will**.
그들이 또 조깅을 할까요? 네, 그럴 거예요.

−

Will she **help** Olive? No, **she will not (won't)**.
그녀가 Olive를 도울까요? 아니요, 그러지 않을 거예요.

Will he **call** back? No, **he will not (won't)**.
그가 다시 전화할까요? 아니요, 그러지 않을 거예요.

Will we **finish** the job? No, **we will not (won't)**.
우리가 일을 끝내게 될까요? 아니요, 그러지 않을 거예요.

Communication situations

Read the following dialogues between a couple of friends – Olive and Alfie – talking about health issues.

Hi, what's up? Oh, you look a bit worried. What's wrong?

Dialogue 1

Alfie: Hi, I'm not worried. I just feel sick.

Olive: Yeah, you look miserable.

Alfie: Well, thank you very much.

Olive: Have you got a high temperature?

Alfie: No, but I've got a cough.

Olive: You should take some cough medicine and in two days you'll be fine.

---

worried 걱정하는 | cough 기침

Dialogue 2

Alfie: Oh, it's because of my dad.

Olive: Why? Is there something wrong with him?

Alfie: Well, his blood results are bad.

Olive: Oh, it sounds worrying.

Alfie: It does but we are not surprised.

Olive: What do you mean?

Alfie: Well, just look at his lifestyle. He's a heavy smoker, for starters.

Olive: I'm not a doctor but I don't believe smoking is to blame here.

Alfie: His diet is full of junk food. It doesn't help.

Olive: Oh, so I assume it's all about the fat. He should try a vegetarian diet.

Alfie: My father and a vegetarian diet?

Olive: Then why doesn't he try a balanced diet? He should see a good nutritionist.

blood results 혈액 검사 결과 | **It sounds worrying.** 걱정되겠구나. | **heavy smoker** 애연가, 골초 | **for starters** 우선, 먼저 | **blame** 탓하다, 책임으로 보다 | **balanced diet** 균형 잡힌 식사

Dialogue 3

Alfie: Hello. Well, I worry about my brother.

Olive: What's happened?

Alfie: I think he's got food poisoning.

Olive: What makes you think so?

Alfie: Well, if you look at the symptoms …

Olive: And what are the symptoms?

Alfie: Apart from vomiting he's got a high temperature and feels pain in his stomach.

Olive: Oh, then you might be right. You should call a doctor. Dehydration can be a very serious problem.

worry about ~에 대해 걱정하다 | **food poisoning** 식중독 | **What are the symptoms?** 증상이 어떤데?

Dialogue 4

Alfie: I know. I'm shivering.

Olive: Have you got a temperature?

Alfie: Yes, I always have a temperature when I have the shakes.

Olive: Oh, I'm sorry to hear that. Do you also have a headache or sore throat?

Alfie: I have the whole set: shivers, a temperature, a headache and a sore throat.

Olive: You should visit a doctor.

Alfie: I'm on my way there now.

Olive: Good luck and get well soon!

shiver (몸을) 떨다 | **I have the shakes.** 오한이 나. | **headache** 두통 | **sore throat** 목 아픔 | **I'm on my way.** 가는 길이야.

Vocabulary plus

allergic to	~에 알레르기가 있는	low in fat	저지방의
amazingly	놀랄 만큼, 굉장히	must	꼭 봐야[해야] 하는 것; 필수품
anyway	그래도	right as rain	아주 건강한
as stubborn as an ox	고집이 황소고집인	see a doctor	병원에 가다
break up (with)	(~와) 헤어지다, 결별하다	swollen	부어오른
cold	감기; 추운	tablet	알약, 정제
get over	(사랑했던 사람을) 잊다	take some pills	알약을 복용하다
GP (general practitioner)	일반 개업의, 가정의	take up	~을 시작하다
hay fever	건초열	the sooner the better	빠를수록 좋다
home-made recipes	가정식 요리법	There are plenty more fish in the sea.	세상에 남자[여자]는 많아.
I'm cold.	추워., 오한이 들어.	wait for	~을 기다리다
in my opinion	내 생각에는, 내 의견으로는	worse and worse	점점 더 나쁜
listen to	~의 말을 귀담아듣다		

Cultural tips

Did you know that …?

When you are at a party, you may find yourself in a situation where you want to make a toast. There are several expressions that you can use: "Cheers!", "To your health!" or "Chin-chin" are very common; as well as "Bottoms up!" or "Down the hatch!", which, however, are much more informal. You can also use a person's name in your toast, for example: "To Olive, my dear friend!".

Scene 11

Film dialogue and vocabulary

Read the dialogue between Olive (O) and the client (C). Check the list of words and phrases below.

I've unlocked the door. I'm in.

O: I'm looking at the painting right now. Okay, let me just …

C: Olive, stop! The plan has changed.

O: What? Are you out of your mind?

C: Behind the painting there is a safe deposit box. I want you to break into it and take the documents that are inside.

O: We've agreed on something else! There is no time!

C: Do it or I'll send Kirsch your mother's current address in San Fernando, California. You're out of his reach now but maybe killing your mum will put him in a better mood.

Vocabulary

unlock	(문 등의) 자물쇠를 열다	agree (on)	(~에) 합의하다
plan	계획	or	안 그러면
change	변경되다, 바뀌다	current	현재의
be out of one's mind	미치다, 정신이 나가다	address	주소
behind	~ 뒤에	be out of (one's) reach	(~의) 힘이 미치지 않는 곳에 있다
box	상자, 함		
safe deposit box	금고	kill	죽이다, 살해하다
document	서류, 문서	put in a good mood	기분 좋게 하다

level A1

Read the dialogue between a bodyguard, Murray (M) and Olive (O). Check the list of words and phrases below.

She hasn't stolen the painting!

Olive, I'm so glad you haven't left the party yet. ... Guy, the handcuffs!

Stop, or I'll shoot you!

Vocabulary		
	yet	아직
	handcuffs	수갑
	stop	멈추다, 서다
	shoot	쏘다

Grammar explanations

동사의 원형, 과거형, 과거분사형

do	did	done
동사 원형	과거형	과거분사형

현재완료

have/has + 과거분사

단수

I **have** work**ed** (I**'ve** work**ed**) on this project for many days.
저는 며칠째 이 프로젝트를 진행하고 있어요.

You **have** prepar**ed** (you**'ve** prepar**ed**) a delicious supper, Jessica.
맛있는 저녁을 준비했군요, Jessica.

Olive **has been** (she**'s been**) in danger many times in her short life.
Olive는 짧은 인생 동안 여러 번 위험에 빠졌어요.

Oh no, it **has broken** (it**'s broken**). I'll have to buy a new camera.
이런, 고장이 났어요. 새 카메라를 사야겠어요.

복수

We **have had** (we**'ve had**) many guests so far this year.
우리는 올해 지금까지 많은 손님을 받았어요.

You **have seen** (you**'ve seen**) my precious painting.
당신들은 제 귀중한 그림을 본 적이 있어요.

The bodyguards **have** stop**ped** (they**'ve** stop**ped**) Olive. She can't go further.
경호원들이 Olive를 제지했어요. 그녀는 더 이상 갈 수가 없어요.

과거 vs. 현재완료

과거

→ 과거에 종료된 행동

I **was** in Old Berry **last summer**.
저는 지난여름 Old Berry에 있었습니다.
(지난여름은 과거이고 체류 기간은 끝남)

David **didn't react** in the pub **a week ago**.
David는 일주일 전에 술집에서 대응하지 않았습니다.
(일주일 전이라 함은 지난주를 뜻함)

현재완료

→ 현재에도 진행 중인 행동

David **has been** a policeman **since 2012**.
David는 2012년부터 경찰이었습니다.
(그는 여전히 경찰이며 since는 상황이 시작된 시점을 나타냄)

I **have been** in Old Berry **for a few days**.
저는 며칠째 Old Berry에 있습니다.
(며칠 전에 도착해서 여전히 체류 중이며 for는 기간을 나타냄)

과거

→ 과거에 순차적으로 일어난 행동

He **came** in, **turned** the light on and **looked** around.
그는 들어와서 불을 켜고 주위를 둘러보았습니다.

→ 과거의 특정 시점에 이루어진 행동

There **was** a lovely party at the Campbells **in 2012**.
2012년에 Campbell 저택에서 멋진 파티가 열렸습니다.

→ 사망한 사람의 경험 및 업적

Charles Dickens **visited** the United States and Canada.
찰스 디킨스는 미국과 캐나다를 방문했습니다.

Jane Austen **wrote** six novels.
제인 오스틴은 여섯 편의 소설을 썼습니다

현재완료

→ 과거에 시작되어 현재까지 계속되는 행동

I'**ve unlocked** the door. I'm in.
제가 잠겨 있던 문을 열었어요. 지금 안에 있어요.

→ 과거의 불특정 시점에 이루어진 행동

We **have seen** this film **before**.
우리는 전에 이 영화를 보았어요.

There **haven't been** many tourists in the town **recently**.
최근에는 마을에 관광객들이 많지 않아요.

→ 살아 있는 사람의 경험 및 업적

I **have visited** most of the countries in Europe.
저는 유럽 대부분의 나라에 가 봤어요.

Zadie Smith **has written** four novels.
제이디 스미스는 네 편의 소설을 썼습니다.

과거와 어울리는 시간 표현 vs. 현재완료와 어울리는 시간 표현

과거

yesterday
last night / **last** Friday / **last** week
2 days **ago** / a month **ago** / 5 years **ago**
in August / **in** 1994 / **in** 2012 / **in** my childhood
when I was young / **when** I was 20

현재완료

today
this week / **this** month / **this** year
since May / **since** Christmas / **since** 2011
for two days / **for** a week / **for** a year
lately / **recently**

규칙 동사의 과거분사

규칙 동사: 과거형 = 과거분사형

watch → watch**ed**
kill → kill**ed**
agree → agree**d**

! enjo**y** → enjoy**ed** (모음 + y = ed)
! sta**y** → stay**ed** (모음 + y = ed)
! stud**y** → stud**ied** (자음 + y = ied)

불규칙 동사의 과거분사

원형	과거형	과거분사형
be	was/were	been
break	broke	broken
buy	bought	bought
cut	cut	cut
come	came	come
cut	cut	cut
do	did	done
drink	drank	drunk
drive	drove	driven
eat	ate	eaten
fly	flew	flown
get	got	got
give	gave	given
go	went	gone

원형	과거형	과거분사형
have	had	had
hit	hit	hit
leave	left	left
make	made	made
meet	met	met
pay	paid	paid
run	ran	run
see	saw	seen
sleep	slept	slept
speak	spoke	spoken
steal	stole	stolen
swim	swam	swum
take	took	taken
think	thought	thought
write	wrote	written

현재완료의 부정문

have not (haven't) + 과거분사
has not (hasn't) + 과거분사

Olive **hasn't seen** the painting yet. Olive는 아직 그 그림을 보지 못했어요.
We **haven't jogged** this week. 우리는 이번 주에 조깅을 하지 않았어요.
I **haven't talked** to Robert for many days. 저는 며칠째 Robert와 이야기하지 않았어요.
I'm glad you **haven't left** yet. 당신이 아직 떠나지 않아서 다행이에요.

현재완료의 의문문과 대답

Have + I/you/we/you/they + 과거분사?
Has + he/she/it + 과거분사?

Yes, I/you/we/you/they **have.**
No, I/you/we/you/they **have not (haven't).**
Yes, he/she/it **has.**
No, he/she/it **has not (hasn't).**

Have you **met** my mother?
저희 어머니를 만난 적이 있나요?

Has Robert **shot** a man?
Robert가 사람을 쐈나요?

Have we **agreed** to steal the painting or the documents?
우리가 그림이나 문서를 훔치기로 합의를 했나요?

Has Robert noticed Olive?
– **Yes,** he **has**.
Robert가 Olive를 알아보았나요? – 네, 그랬어요.

Have you met my mother?
– **No,** I **haven't**.
저희 어머니를 만난 적이 있나요? – 아니요, 없어요.

명령문

+

동사 원형 + ... !

Leave it ! 놔두세요!
Call me ! 제게 전화하세요!
Stop, or I'll shoot you !
거기서, 안 그러면 쏘겠다!

−

Do not (don't) + 동사 원형 + ... !

Do not (Don't) touch the glass ! 유리잔을 만지지 마세요!
Do not (Don't) enter the building ! 건물에 들어가지 마세요!
Do not (Don't) listen to him ! 그의 말을 듣지 마세요!

Communication situations

Read the following dialogues between the boss of a company specialising in organizing cultural events and his assistant.

It's finally May. We've been on the event market for half a year now, but summer is our chance to really spread our wings!

Dialogue 1

Boss: OK. Then could you make a list of all the event application deadlines?

Assistant: I have already done that.

Boss: Really? You are amazing!

Assistant: First comes the LIFT Festival in June, then Camden Festival in July, and Notting Hill Carnival in the second half of August.

Boss: Apply to all of them.

Assistant: Are you sure? They are all quite time-consuming in terms of preparation.

Boss: Well, we have to aim high if we want to make a name for ourselves.

Assistant: Time will tell if you're right, I guess.

---

finally 드디어, 마침내 | **spread one's wings** ~의 능력을 충분히 발휘하다 | **application deadline** 신청 마감일 | **apply to** ~에 신청하다, 지원하다 | **in terms of** ~의 면에서, ~에 관하여 | **time-consuming** 시간이 걸리는 | **aim high** 목표를 높게 잡다 | **make a name for** 이름을 알리다, 유명해지다 | **Time will tell.** 시간이 지나면 알게 되겠죠.

Dialogue 2

Boss: Could you write me a memo about the events we discussed in our business meeting?

Assistant: Of course. When do you want to have it?

Boss: Just let me know when we can talk it over.

Assistant: Shall I focus on something in particular?

Boss: Concentrate on big, international theatre festivals.

Assistant: You mean – something like the one in Edinburgh?

Boss: Yes, that's exactly what I have in mind!

Assistant: OK. I'll start with making a list of multicultural events and see where it takes us.

---

memo 메모 | talk something over ~에 대해 논의하다 | focus on ~에 집중하다, 초점을 맞추다 | in particular 특히, 특별히 | have in mind 생각하다, 염두에 두다

Dialogue 3

Boss: As far as I can remember, the painting exhibition takes place in June and the concert in July.

Assistant: Yes, that's correct.

Boss: Let's take care of the exhibition first.

Assistant: And what are we exhibiting – the paintings or the sculptures? Have you decided yet?

Boss: Yes, I have. We are going to do the sculpture exhibition.

Assistant: So what's next?

Boss: Set up a meeting with the artists and the city council representatives.

Assistant: What will be the subject of this meeting?

Boss: Good question. Prepare the agenda first.

Assistant: Of course, I will. But I'd like you to have a look at it before I send it, all right?

Boss: Include the venue, the date and the city council's subsidy, for starters.

Assistant: All right, will do.

---

take care of ~을 처리하다; ~을 돌보다 | sculpture exhibition 조각전 | set up a meeting 회의를 잡다 | city council 시의회 | subject 주제 | venue 장소 | subsidy 보조금

Vocabulary plus

advertising space	광고 지면
basics	기초, 기초적인 것들
Care to elaborate?	더 자세히 설명해 줄래요?
easy-peasy	아주 쉬운
fair	박람회
fit in with	~와 어울리다
follow	따르다
fresh and edgy	신선하고 독특한
gain	얻다
get down to business	본론으로 들어가다
go smoothly	순조롭게 진행되다
Good point.	좋은 지적이에요.
if I remember correctly	제 기억이 맞다면
I'm on it.	제가 처리할게요.
it seems	~인 것처럼 보인다
leave out	~을 빼다, 배제하다
make something up	(이야기 등을) 지어내다
moody	감정기복이 심한
much more challenging	훨씬 더 어려운
out of this world	이 세상 것이 아닌, 너무도 훌륭한
out-of-space ideas	기상천외한 생각
parties	관계자들, 당사자들; 정당들
require	요하다, 요구하다
stand out	돋보이다, 눈에 띄다
standard form	표준 서식
take a closer look	자세히 살펴보다
That sounds quite unwise.	별로 현명한 것 같지 않은데요.
to be honest	솔직히 말하자면
True.	맞아요.
world-famous	세계적으로 유명한
worthwhile	훌륭한, 가치 있는

Cultural tips

Did you know that ...?

The Edinburgh Festival is a collective term for the numerous arts and cultural festivals that take place each summer, mostly in August, in Edinburgh, Scotland.

The photo shows the city of Edinburgh.

Scene 12

Film dialogue and vocabulary

Read the dialogue between Murray (M) and David (D). Check the list of words and phrases below.

Such a pity, Olive. I wanted us to be good friends.

D: Drop your gun!

M: Constable Owen, you have to arrest this woman! She's just stolen some very important business documents.

D: Mr Murray, you have to drop your gun! Now!

M: She is a dangerous criminal! She attacked my employees and she drugged my son.

D: Olive, did you?

Vocabulary				
	It's (such) a pity!	(정말) 안타깝군!	arrest	체포하다
	drop	내려놓다, 떨어뜨리다	attack	공격하다
	gun	총	employee	직원
	constable	순경, 경관	drug	약[마취제]을 먹이다

level A1

Read the dialogue between David (D) and Olive (O). Check the list of words and phrases below.

> We have to report this! What we did ... I can't do things like that! I'm a policeman!

> David, you must calm down!

D: Olive, who the hell are you? Is your name really Olive? Are you really a criminal?

O: Where is your goddamn car? Yes, David, I'm a criminal. I steal works of art. Sometimes I hurt people, but I never murder them.

D: What about me? What was my job in your plan?

O: The problem is I like you, David. More than I've liked anyone for a long time. So I didn't want to make trouble for you.

Vocabulary				
report	신고하다, 보고하다	sometimes	가끔
must	~해야 한다	hurt	해치다, 다치게 하다
calm down	진정하다	never	절대 ~ 않다
Who the hell?	대체 누구죠?	murder	죽이다, 살인하다
goddamn	빌어먹을	problem	문제
car	자동차	like	좋아하다
work of art	미술품	long	오랜, 긴

level A1 Scene 12

Grammar explanations

의무의 의미를 나타내는 have to / has to

단수

I've accepted the job so I **have to** steal the painting.
일을 수락했기 때문에 저는 그림을 훔쳐야 해요.

You **have to** understand who I am and what I do.
당신은 제가 누구인지, 제가 무엇을 하는지 이해해야 해요.

She **has to** accept the plan. She **has to** think about it.
그녀는 계획을 받아들여야 해요. 그에 대해 생각해봐야 해요.

Mr Murray has got a gun. David **has to** arrest him. That's the law.
Murray 씨는 총을 가지고 있어요. David는 그를 체포해야 하죠. 그것이 법이에요.

This nightmare **has to** be over ...
이 악몽은 끝나야 해요…

복수

There is no time. We **have to** run now.
시간이 없어요. 지금 뛰어야 해요.

You **have to** take the documents from her. Run after her!
당신들은 그녀에게서 문서를 빼앗아야 해요. 그녀를 뒤쫓아요!

Robert and his people **have to** report the theft to the police.
Robert와 그의 부하들은 도난 사건을 경찰에 신고해야 해요.

→ 충고나 권고의 의미를 나타내는 경우

Olive, I know you don't like the change but you **have to** accept it.
Olive, 당신이 바뀐 점을 좋아하지 않는다는 점은 알고 있지만 받아들여야 해요.

have to / has to가 들어간 의문문과 대답

단수

Do I **have to** do the job?
제가 그 일을 해야 하나요?

Yes, I do. I don't want my mother to be in danger.
네, 그래요. 저는 어머니가 위험에 빠지는 것을 원치 않아요.

Do you **have to** hurt people?
당신은 사람들을 다치게 해야 하나요?

Yes, I do. Sometimes I **have to** … but I never murder them.
네, 그래요. 가끔 다치게 해야 하죠… 하지만 절대 살인은 안 해요.

Does he always **have to** be nice?
그가 항상 친절해야 하나요?

No, he does not (he doesn't). He **has to** be firm with criminals.
아니요, 그렇지 않아요. 범죄자들에게는 단호해야 하죠.

Does she **have to** drag David?
그녀가 David를 끌고 가야 하나요?

Yes, she does. She's got no time for talks. She **has to** run away.
네, 그래요. 이야기를 할 시간이 없어요. 그녀는 도망쳐야 해요.

Does the painting **have to** be in the gallery?
그 그림은 화랑에 있어야 하나요?

Yes, it does. It's very valuable. It needs special conditions like temperature and humidity.
네, 그래요. 그것은 매우 귀한 거예요. 온도와 습도와 같은 특별한 조건이 필요해요.

복수

David, do we **have to** talk right now?
David, 우리가 지금 이야기를 해야 하나요?

No, we don't. We don't have to talk but I **have to** arrest you and Robert.
아니요, 그렇지 않아요. 이야기를 할 필요는 없고, 저는 당신과 Robert를 체포해야 해요.

Do you **have to** stand here?
당신들은 여기에 서 있어야 하나요?

No, you don't. You **have to** catch her and take the documents!
아니요, 그렇지 않아요. 당신들은 그녀를 잡아서 문서를 빼앗아야 해요!

Do they **have to** report it to the police?
그들이 그것을 경찰에 신고해야 하나요?

Yes, they do. But Olive doesn't want to do it.
네, 그래요. 하지만 Olive는 그렇게 하는 것을 원하지 않죠.

허가 및 금지의 의미를 나타내는 can/can't

단수

I **can** call my mother but I **can't** visit her. It's too risky.
어머니에게 전화할 수는 있지만 방문을 해서는 안 돼요. 그건 너무 위험해요.

You **can** have any job you want but you **can't** hurt people.
당신은 얼마든지 원하는 직업을 가질 수 있지만 사람들을 다치게 해서는 안 돼요.

David **can** arrest criminals but he **can't** do it without proof.
David는 범죄자를 체포할 수 있지만 증거 없이 그렇게 해서는 안 돼요.

Jessica **can** say silly things to Olive but she **can't** make her fall in love with David.
Jessica가 Olive에게 주책스러운 말을 할 수는 있지만 그녀가 David를 사랑하도록 만들어서는 안 돼요.

Robert **can** shoot Olive and David but … the film **can't** finish like that.
Robert가 Olive와 David를 쏠 수는 있지만… 영화가 그렇게 끝나서는 안 돼요.

복수

We **can** run after Olive but we **can't** hurt her. It's against the law.
우리가 Olive를 뒤쫓을 수는 있지만 그녀를 다치게 해서는 안 돼요. 그건 위법이에요.

You **can** attack her but you **can't** destroy the documents. They are very important.
당신들은 그녀를 공격할 수 있지만 서류를 없애서는 안 돼요. 그 서류는 매우 중요하거든요.

David and Olive **can** say a few words but they **can't** talk too long. Olive has to run away.
David와 Olive가 몇 마디 말을 나눌 수는 있겠지만 너무 오래 이야기해서는 안 돼요. Olive는 도망쳐야 해요.

must

→ 당위의 의미를 나타내는 경우

I **must steal** the painting at tomorrow's party. That's my only chance.
저는 내일 파티에서 그림을 훔쳐야 해요. 그때가 유일한 기회예요.

I **must leave** now. The bodyguards can't see me.
저는 지금 떠나야 해요. 경호원들이 저를 볼 수 없어요.

You **must calm** down. Or the bad guys will find us.
당신은 진정해야 해요. 안 그러면 악당들이 우리를 발견할 거예요.

She **must do** the job. She wants her mum to be safe.
그녀는 그 일을 해야 해요. 그녀는 어머니가 안전하기를 바라니까요.

David **must arrest** Olive. He knows it's his duty.
David는 Olive를 체포해야 해요. 그는 그것이 자신의 임무라는 것을 알아요.

Everything **must work** in my plan. Or I'll be in big trouble.
모든 것이 제 계획대로 되어야 해요. 그렇지 않으면 저는 곤경에 빠질 거예요.

→ 권고의 의미를 나타내는 경우

You **must** **buy** this dress. It's perfect for you.
당신은 이 드레스를 사야 해요. 정말 잘 어울려요.

We **must** **visit** Old Berry and see the stone circles.
우리는 Old Berry를 방문해서 스톤 서클을 봐야 해요.

Have you seen the cathedral? No? Oh, you **must** **see** it, it's really impressive!
그 성당을 본 적이 있나요? 없어요? 오, 반드시 봐야 해요. 정말 인상적이거든요!

Skyfall is one of the best James Bond films. You **must** **watch** it!
스카이폴은 제임스 본드 영화 중 최고예요. 반드시 봐야 해요!

I really love live concerts. You **must** **go** with me one day!
저는 라이브 콘서트를 정말 좋아해요. 언제 한번 저와 같이 보러 가요!

Communication situations

Read the following dialogues between a man and a woman travelling by car.

Listen, I'm driving, looking at the road signs and reading a map. I can't be paying attention to all your stories as well.

Dialogue 1

Woman: So turn on the satnav.

Man: I don't trust this device. It's stupid.

Woman: I could say exactly the same about you right now.

Man: Believe it or not but when there are roadworks on the way, it goes crazy.

Woman: But you have never tried it!

Man: I don't have to and I don't intend to.

Woman: Sometimes you can be really narrow-minded, you know?

Man: No, I'm not. I just ... Hmm, I just stick to my principles.

---

road signs 도로 표지판 I **pay attention** 신경 쓰다, 주의를 기울이다 I **turn on** ~을 켜다 I **roadworks** 도로 공사 I **go crazy** 이상해지다, 미치다 I **narrow-minded** 속이 좁은 I **stick to** ~을 고수하다, 굳게 지키다 I **principles** 원칙

Dialogue 2

Woman: OK. Keep driving and I'll be learning the road signs for my driving licence.

Man: That's a very good idea. Let's start. What does this sign mean?

Woman: Which one?

Man: The red circle with a white background and a black icon.

Woman: Well, if there is a number inside, it shows the speed limit.

Man: Good. And if it's crossed?

Woman: The speed limit is no longer valid.

Man: Well done!

---

driving licence 운전면허 | **background** 바탕, 배경 | **speed limit** 제한 속도 | **crossed (out)** 선을 긋다, 선을 그어 지우다 | **no longer valid** 더는 유효하지 않은

Dialogue 3

Woman: Then stop, pull over and let's park over there.

Man: Why?

Woman: Because we've come to the city centre and we can't go on in a car.

Man: OK. Right. So how are we going to do our sightseeing?

Woman: I think the subway will be the fastest.

Man: First of all, it's called the Tube here, and second of all, we won't see anything from it.

Woman: Right ... So I suggest a bus.

Man: Yeah, I know, you want to experience "the queue".

Woman: Yes, and also buying a ticket from the driver.

Man: You are funny. But OK, let's do it. Let's take a bus.

---

pull over 길가에 차를 세우다 | **sightseeing** 관광 | **queue** 줄

Vocabulary plus

bend	(방향이) 휘어지다; (방향을) 틀다	no turning	유턴 금지
		No way!	말도 안 돼!
double-decker	이층 버스	old-fashioned	구식의, 옛날식의
give way	양보하다	operate	(기계 등을) 움직이다, 운전하다; 작동하다
go for it	한번 해보다		
go with the times	시대의 흐름을 따르다	precise	정확한, 정밀한
I don't care.	알게 뭐야., 상관없어.	reach the destination	목적지에 도달하다
I'm not really eager to ...	나는 그다지 ~하고 싶지 않다	reliable	믿을 수 있는
		reset the settings	설정을 초기화하다
make sure	반드시 ~하게 하다	to the left	왼쪽으로
manual	수동의; 설명서	user-friendly	사용하기 편한
no entry	출입 금지	You have a point.	일리 있는 말이네요.
no overtaking	추월 금지		

Cultural tips

Did you know that ...?

Park-and-ride are parking lots with public transport connections that allow people who go to city centres to leave their cars and transfer to a bus or train to continue their journey. Park-and-rides are generally located in the suburbs of large cities. The name is abbreviated to "P+R" on road signs in the UK. Park-and-rides began in the 1960s in the UK, with the first one in Oxford.

Translation

Scene 1

Film dialogue and vocabulary p. 8~11

A: 그녀의 이름은 가브리엘라 아퀼라, A-G-U-I-L-A-R.

A: 국적은 미국. 나이는 26세. 숙련된 미술품 절도범입니다. 보스는 디터 커쉬. 하지만 둘 사이에 일이 꼬이는 바람에 그녀는 현상 수배 중입니다. 혼자에 돈도 떨어졌죠. 제가 봤을 땐 그녀가 적임자입니다!

C: 너무 어리지만⋯ 괜찮군!

C: 아퀼라 씨? 가브리엘라 아퀼라 씨? 듣고 있습니까?

G: 누구시죠?

C: 아퀼라 씨, 미술품⋯ 뭐라고 하나⋯?

G: 컨설턴트요. 미술품 컨설턴트예요.

C: 컨설턴트? 그래, 재미있군! 난 새 의뢰인이오. 좋은 제안을 하나 하지.

> **accept**

G: 좋아요! 어떤 일이죠?

C: 쉽소. 영국에서 하는 일이지.

G: 영국? 그건 좋은데 제가⋯

C: 곤경에 빠졌지. JFK공항 물품 보관함에 여권이 있소. 당신 사진이 붙어 있지. 새 이름은⋯ 올리브 그린.

> **don't accept**

G: 관심 없어요. 휴가 중이에요.

   (⋯)

C: 아퀼라 씨? 당신은 휴가 중이 아니라 브루클린 그린우드가 9번지의 아파트에 있소. 곤경에 빠졌고.

G: 제가요?

C: 그렇소! 당신 보스 커쉬가 감옥에 있지⋯ 당신 때문에.

G: 살인을 해서 감옥에 간 거예요.

C: 하지만 당신 탓이라 그의 부하들에게 쫓기고 있잖소! 지금 당신에게 미국은 아주 위험해. 하지만 벗어날 방법은 있소!

G: 무슨 방법요?

C: JFK공항 물품 보관함에 여권이 있소. 당신 사진이 붙어 있지. 새 이름은⋯ 올리브 그린.

G: 알았어요! 그만해요! 어떤 일인데요?

Olive Green

Communication situations   p. 14~15

Olive: 안녕하세요, 제 이름은 올리브 그린이에요. 당신의 이름은 무엇인가요?

Dialogue 1

Peter: 안녕하세요, 제 이름은 피터예요.

Olive: 오늘 기분이 어떠세요?

Peter: 좋아요, 고마워요. 당신은요?

Olive: 저도 좋아요. 고맙습니다. 어디에서 오셨어요?

Peter: 저는 인도에서 왔어요.

Olive: 그렇다면 아시아 출신이군요. 휴대폰이 있겠네요. 휴대폰 번호가 어떻게 되죠?

Peter: 03 03 88 56이에요.

Olive: 다시 한번 말씀해 주시겠어요?

Peter: 물론이죠. 03 03 88 56이에요.

Olive: 네, 이제 제대로 알아들었어요. 고마워요.

Dialogue 2

James: 안녕하세요, 저는 제임스예요.

Olive: 만나서 반가워요. 어디에서 오셨어요?

James: 유럽에서 왔어요.

Olive: 아, 유럽 사람들은 제게 늘 흥미로워요. 저는 미국인이에요. 당신은요? 독일인인가요, 아니면 프랑스인?

James: 아니요, 저는 폴란드인이에요.

Olive: 그러면 거기서는 어떤 일 하세요?

James: 저는 교사예요.

Olive: 그렇다면 학교에서 일하시는군요. 제가 찾아가도 될까요?

James: 네, 찾아오셔도 돼요. 괜찮아요.

Olive: 이메일 주소가 어떻게 되세요?

James: 제 이메일은 EVE@YAHOO.COM이에요.

Olive: 고마워요. 곧 연락해요.

Dialogue 3

Peter: 안녕하세요, 제 이름은 피터예요.

Olive: 오늘 기분이 어떠세요?

Peter: 꽤 좋아요. 당신은요?

Olive: 좋아요, 고마워요. 어디서 오셨나요?

Peter: 저는 캘리포니아에서 왔어요.

Olive: 정말이에요? 저도 마찬가지예요!

Peter: 정말 신기하네요!

Olive: 그럼 무슨 일 하세요?

Peter: 저는 의사예요.

Olive: 주소는요?

Peter: 저는 North Road 5번가에 살아요.

Scene 2

Film dialogue and vocabulary p. 18~19

올드 베리라는 마을이오. 작고 예쁜 마을로 특별할 게 없지.

마을 주변에 돌이 원형으로 늘어서 있소. 대외적으로는 그게 당신이 온 이유요.

… 올리브 그린은 미국에서 온 고고학 전공 학생이니까.

여기는 캠벨 저택. 22개의 침실과 대형 서재, 정원이 있소.

이 사람은 로버트 머리. 나이, 55세. 직업은 사업가. 영악하고 위험한 사람이지.

로버트 머리의 아들, 커티스. 나이는 28세. 직업은 없지만 중요한 관심사가 두 개 있소. 술과 여자.

이 사람은 베아트리스 머리. 결혼 전 성은 캠벨. 커티스의 어머니이자 로버트의 아내지. 나이는 46세. 주부고 취미는 정원 가꾸기.

이 그림들은 잘 알려진 머리의 수집품이지.

이 그림은 "엉겅퀴"로 인상파 걸작이오. 시가 2천5백만 내지 3천만 파운드지… 당신의 임무는 이 그림을 훔쳐 주는 거요.

Communication situations p. 22~24

A: 가족이 있나요?

Dialogue 1

B: 네, 있어요.

A: 형제나 자매 있어요?

B: 네, 오빠 하나, 언니 하나가 있어요.

A: 그분들은 어디에 사나요?

B: 오빠는 영국에 살아요.

A: 그러면 언니는요?

B: 언니는 캐나다에 살아요.

Dialogue 2

B: 음, 곤란하네요.
A: 무슨 뜻이죠? 부모님께서 돌아가셨나요?
B: 아니요, 그건 아닌데, 별로 사이가 좋지 않거든요.
A: 그렇군요. 그러면 형제자매는 있나요?
B: 아니요, 없어요. 하지만 친구는 많아요.

Dialogue 3

B: 그 이야기는 하고 싶지 않아요.
A: 에이, 그러지 말고요. 몇 마디라도 해 보세요. 알았죠? 자, 가족이 있나요?
B: 네, 있어요.
A: 형제나 자매가 있나요?
B: 네, 남동생이 하나 있어요.
A: 남동생은 어디에 살아요?
B: 남동생은 부모님과 함께 살고 있어요.

Dialogue 4

B: 음, 곤란하네요.
A: 무슨 뜻이죠? 부모님께서 돌아가셨나요?
B: 어머니와 아버지는 돌아가셨어요.
A: 그러면 부모님의 형제나 자매는요?
B: 외삼촌은 뉴욕에 살고 계세요.
A: 어떤 일을 하시나요?
B: 외삼촌은 미술품 컨설턴트예요.

Scene 3

Film dialogue and vocabulary p. 26~27

J: 어서 와요. 미안해요, 그거 고장 났어요!
O: 안녕하세요. 전 올리브 그린이에요. 방을 예약했는데요.
J: 네, 맞아요. 여기에 적어뒀어요. 다음 주 금요일까지 있을 거죠? 미안해요. 내 정신 좀 봐! 난 제시카, 여기 주인이에요. (…)
O: 왜요?
J: 아니에요. 미혼이죠?
O: 뭐라고요?

J: 미혼 맞죠?

D: 어머니 말은 신경 쓰지 마세요. 제 짝을 찾아주려는 거예요. 안녕하세요, 데이비드예요. 반가워요.

O: 전 올리브예요. 저도 반가워요.

J: 데이비드, 짐 좀 방까지 가져다드리렴.

D: 무거운데요! 안에 뭐가 든 거죠? 무기랑 폭탄요? (…) 농담이에요.

💬
D: 가시죠. 5호실로.

Communication situations   p. 30~31

💬
Receptionist: 안녕하세요. Grand 호텔에 오신 것을 환영합니다. 무엇을 도와드릴까요?

Dialogue 1

Guest: 안녕하세요. 이 호텔의 객실 하나를 예약했는데요.

Receptionist: 성함이 어떻게 되세요?

Guest: 사라 존스예요.

Receptionist: 잠시만 기다려 주십시오. 아 네, 존스 씨. 저희 호텔에 오신 것을 환영합니다. 여기 키 받으세요.

Guest: 고마워요.

Receptionist: 더 필요한 것 있으십니까?

Guest: 네. 이곳에 운동 시설이 있나요?

Receptionist: 네, 있습니다. 수영장과 사우나, 그리고 체육관이 있습니다.

Guest: 몇 시에 여나요?

Receptionist: 모든 시설은 오전 9시부터 오후 9시 30분까지 엽니다.

Guest: 식당은 몇 시에 여나요?

Receptionist: 아침 식사는 6시 30분부터 10시까지 제공합니다. 점심 식사는 12시부터 오후 4시까지고, 식당은 오후 10시 30분까지 엽니다.

Guest: 그렇군요. 도와주셔서 감사합니다.

Receptionist: 천만에요.

Dialogue 2

Guest: 안녕하세요. 객실을 예약하고 싶은데요.

Receptionist: 싱글룸으로 하시겠습니까, 더블룸으로 하시겠습니까?

Guest: 싱글룸을 예약하고 싶어요.

Receptionist: 체크인은 언제 하시겠습니까?

Guest: 화요일 오전에요.

Receptionist: 몇 시에 하시겠습니까?

Guest: 오전 10시 30분쯤에 체크인하고 싶어요.

Receptionist: 알겠습니다. 감사합니다. 몇 박 하시겠습니까?

Guest: 1박요.

Receptionist: 그러면 결제는 어떻게 하시겠습니까? 신용 카드로 하시겠습니까, 현금으로 하시겠습니까?

Guest: 아직 모르겠어요.

Receptionist: 네, 괜찮습니다. 나중에 결정하셔도 됩니다.

Dialogue 3

Guest: 안녕하세요, 예약을 변경하고 싶은데요.

Receptionist: 물론이지요, 문제없습니다. 성함을 말씀해 주시겠습니까?

Guest: 스미스 부부로 예약했어요.

Receptionist: 손님의 예약은 5월 3일 수요일에 시작하고, 체크아웃은 5월 5일 금요일이네요. 무엇을 변경하시겠습니까?

Guest: 목요일에 체크인하고 싶어요.

Receptionist: 그러시군요. 확인해 드리겠습니다. 5월 4일 목요일에 체크인하셔서 5월 5일에 체크아웃입니다. 맞습니까?

Guest: 네, 완벽해요. 고마워요.

Receptionist: 더 필요한 것 있으십니까?

Guest: 아뇨, 그게 다예요. 감사합니다.

Scene 4

Film dialogue and vocabulary   p. 34~35

J: 올리브, 왔어요? 옷 갈아입고 저녁 먹어요.

O: 괜찮아요. 배 안 고파요.

J: 고프잖아요. 내 말 들어요. 직접 만든 수프도 준비했어요.

O: 절 위해서요?

J: 와서 여기 앉아요, 올리브.

O: 고맙습니다. 와, 맛있겠는데요.

J: 고마워요. 맘껏 먹어요! (…)

J: 난 그만 자러 갈 테니까 둘이 남아서 와인 좀 더 마셔요.

D: 와인 더 드려요?

O: 와인은 묘한 술이죠. 그래도 뭐… 주세요!

D: 말해 봐요. 왜 그렇게 그 돌들에 관심이 많죠? 별 쓸 데도 없고! 예쁘지도 않잖아요. 지지리도 지루한 일 같은데요.

O: 당신은 왜 올드 베리에서 경찰로 일해요? 이 동네에 범죄자가 몇 명이나 있죠? 둘?

D: 절대 아니거든요! 날마다 어려운 사건들을 많이 해결한다고요.

O: 자전거 도난? 음주 운전? 고양이 실종?

D: 고양이 실종은 중대한 일이에요. 고양이를 잃어버린 아이들을 생각해 봐요.

O: 정말 죄송해요. 네, 지역 사회를 위해 중요한 일을 하시네요.

Communication situations   p. 38-39

Olive: 안녕하세요. 집에 계셔서 다행이에요. 배고파 죽겠어요. 먹을 것 있나요?

Dialogue 1

David: 엄마는 항상 우리 먹으라고 점심을 전자레인지에 넣어 두세요.

Olive: 네, 네, 하지만 배가 너무 고파요. 지금 당장 뭔가를 먹어야겠어요.

David: 냉장고에 스파게티가 있어요.

Olive: 전자레인지에 좀 넣어줄래요? 저는 손 좀 씻게요.

David: 치킨 라이스도 있어요.

Olive: 고맙지만, 괜찮아요. 저는 스파게티가 더 좋아요.

Dialogue 2

David: 아뇨, 없는데, 저도 배고파요.

Olive: 그리고 제시카는 아직 여성 단체 모임에 가 있고요. 음, 우리가 뭔가 준비해야겠네요. 뭐 먹고 싶어요?

David: 팬케이크가 먹고 싶어요. 만들 수 있어요?

Olive: 당신이 도와준다면야, 가능하죠. 접시 좀 찾아봅시다.

David: 싱크대 좀 보세요. 모든 게 더럽네요.

Olive: 이런… 누군가는 설거지를 해야겠네요.

David: 저는 설거지가 정말 싫어요.

Olive: 불평 그만하고 일 좀 시작해요.

David: 주방 세제는 어디에 있죠?

Olive: 싱크대 옆에 있을 거예요, 언제나처럼. 물어보기 전에 확인 좀 해 봐요.

Dialogue 3

David: 샌드위치 몇 개와 치킨 샐러드가 있어요.

Olive: 샐러드는 먹고 샌드위치는 싸 가지고 나가요.

David: 나가자고요? 왜요?

Olive: 오늘이 화요일이라, 수영장에 가잖아요. 기억 안 나요?

David: 아, 맞다… 그런데, 정말 다이빙 수업을 시작하고 싶은 거예요?

Olive: 네, 당연하죠. 그럼 당신은 아니에요?

David: 아니에요. 저는 수영이 더 좋아요.

Olive: 음, 그래도 시도는 해 보세요. 마음에 안 들면 그때 수영으로 돌아가도 되잖아요.

Scene 5

Film dialogue and vocabulary   p. 42~43

D: 안녕하세요! 같이 뛸까요?

O: 조깅도 하세요?

D: 그런 셈이죠. 경찰이라 체력 관리해야 하거든요.

O: 좋아요. 실력 좀 보여 줘요. (…)

O: 괜찮아요? 좀 쉴래요?

D: 괜찮아요… 그런데 물 좀 있어요?

O: 썩 나쁜 동네는 아니네요.

D: 왜 이래요! 멋지잖아요! 있을 건 다 있어요. 술집, 지역 센터, 수영장, 게다가 작은 극장도 있어요…

O: 3D도 상영해요? 우리 미국인들은 3D만 보는데.

D: 아뇨, 그건 아니지만… 즐길 거리도 많고 심지어 돈 벌 기회도 있어요… 사람들도 좋고… 올드 베리엔 좋은 사람이 많아요.

O: 네, 저도 몇 명 알아요.

D: 저기, 여기 잠깐 머무르는 건 알지만… 저랑 술 한잔하실래요?

> don't agree

O: 데이비드, 좋은 생각이 아니에요. 프로젝트를 끝내야 해요.

D: 하지만 제가 이 지역 역사에 빠삭해요! 저랑 다니면 프로젝트에 도움이 될 거예요!

O: 그래요? … 그럼 좋아요! … 더 뛸 준비 됐어요?

> agree

O: 제 답은 '예'예요. 하지만 순전히 당신 어머니가 기뻐하는 걸 보고 싶어서예요.

D: 좋아요! 정말 상냥하시네요.

O: 제가 한 "상냥"하죠. 더 뛸 준비 됐어요?

Communication situations   p. 46~47

Olive: 안녕하세요, 데이비드, 저 갈 준비 다 됐어요.

Dialogue 1

David: 잘됐네요. 어디에 가고 싶나요?

Olive: 올드 베리의 밤 문화가 보고 싶어요.

David: 알았어요. 재미있게 놀아 봐요!

Olive: 좋아요! 계획이 어떻게 되나요?

David: 우선, 식당에 가고, 그다음에는 술집에 가거나 로맨틱하게 산책하죠.

Olive: 좋기는 한데 그다지 활동적이지는 않은 것 같아요. 2안도 있나요?

David: 오래된 마을의 야경을 보여 주고 싶어요.

Olive: 오, 멋지네요! 그다음에는요?

David: 영화를 볼까요?

Olive: 그래요. 극장에 가요.

David: 잠깐만요. 저는 극장이 아니라 영화관에 대해 물은 건데요.

Olive: 데이비드, 저도 영화가 보고 싶어요. 뉴욕에서는 '극장'에 간다고 하고 여기 영국에서는, '영화관'이라고 하죠.

Dialogue 2

David: 그건 괜찮은데, 엄마가 아직 준비를 못 하셨어요.

Olive: 어… 당신과 당신 어머니와 함께하는 데이트인가요?

David: 농담이에요! 자, 무엇을 하고 싶나요?

Olive: 올드 베리의 밤 문화가 보고 싶어요.

David: 정확히 뭘 보고 싶은데요?

Olive: 관광 안내 책자에서는 찾아볼 수 없는 것요. 저를 감동시켜 보세요.

David: 기차역을 보여 드릴게요.

Olive: 기차역요? 기차역이 뭐 대단할 게 있나요?

David: 그곳에 아이스 링크와 디스코텍이 있어요.

Olive: 훌륭하군요! 그러면 우리는 무엇을 선택하는 거죠? 디스코텍, 아니면 아이스 스케이트 타기?

David: 디스코텍에 가요.

Olive: 흠, 아니면 아이스 스케이트를 한 시간 탄 다음에 디스코텍에 가는 건 어때요? 제가 아이스 스케이트 타는 걸 정말 좋아하거든요!

David: 좋아요, 안 될 것 없죠.

Dialogue 3

David: 좋아요. 그러면 버스를 타러 가죠.

Olive: 뭐라고요? 버스요?

David: 음, 네. 올드 베리에는 지하철이 없어요.

Olive: 지하도? 아, 지하철을 말하는 거군요. 알았어요, 신경 쓰지 마세요. 차가 있지 않나요?

David: 있는데 고장 났어요.

Olive: 네, 네, 버스 정류장까지 걸어가죠. 얼마나 걸리나요?

David: 택시로는 10분, 걸어서는 30분 넘게요.

Olive: 버스 정류장에 가는 데 택시를 타야 한다니 놀랍네요…

Scene 6

Film dialogue and vocabulary   p. 50~51

Barman: 라거 한 잔 더, 그리고 얼음 넣은 위스키 한 잔 더!

D: 포켓볼까지! 대체 못 하는 게 뭐예요!

B: 데이비드, 운 좋은 줄 알아! 멋진 여자야!

D: 빌, 감옥에 있는 거 아니었어?

B: 너 때문에 갔었지!

D: 어쩌겠어, 빌… 갈만하니까 간 거지!

B: 이름이 뭐야, 예쁜 아가씨? 말수가 적군. 좋은 거지! 난 그런 여자가 좋더라고! 요즘엔 그런 여자 만나기가 쉽지 않거든!

D: 빌, 그만해!

O: 데이트를 하는 게 아니었어요.

O: 이젠 정말 프로젝트를 끝내야 해요. 이럴 시간이…

D: 제가 얼간이라서요?

O: 잘 자요, 데이비드.

Communication situations   p. 54~55

Waiter: 안녕하세요, 손님, 무엇을 도와드릴까요?

Dialogue 1

Client: 여기 테이블을 예약했는데요.

Waiter: 성함을 말씀해 주시겠습니까?

Client: 제 이름은 존 스미스예요.

Waiter: 잠시만 기다려 주십시오. 네, 스미스 씨. 테이블이 마련되어 있습니다. 저와 같이 가시죠. 주문하시겠습니까?

Client: 주방장 특선 요리가 뭐죠?

Waiter: 전채 요리는 토마토 수프, 메인 요리는 으깬 감자와 혼합 샐러드를 곁들인 스테이크, 디저트는 크림을 얹은 딸기입니다.

Client: 메인 요리만 주세요.

Waiter: 알겠습니다. 마실 것도 드릴까요?

Client: 네, 라거 1파인트 주세요.

Waiter: 알겠습니다, 손님. 주문 감사합니다. 금방 가져다드리겠습니다.

Dialogue 2

Client: 두 명 앉을 테이블 부탁해요.

Waiter: 예약하셨습니까?

Client: 아니요, 안 했어요.

Waiter: 죄송하지만 지금 당장은 테이블이 없습니다. 바에서 기다리시겠습니까?

Client: 네, 그럴게요.

Waiter: 저를 따라오십시오. 여기에 앉으십시오. 뭐라도 가져다드릴까요?

Client: 화이트 와인 한 잔 주세요.

Waiter: 드라이한 와인, 약간 드라이한 와인, 아니면 단맛이 나는 와인 중 어느 것으로 하시겠습니까?

Client: 약간 드라이한 와인으로 주세요. 그리고 와인에 대한 계산서도 주시겠어요?

Waiter: 와인은 식사 주문과 함께 계산서에 포함될 것입니다.

Client: 오, 좋네요.

Waiter: 와인 맛있게 드십시오!

Dialogue 3

Client: 한 명 앉을 테이블 부탁해요.

Waiter: 죄송하지만 지금 당장은 테이블이 없습니다. 바에서 기다리시겠습니까?

Client: 아니요, 괜찮아요. 그러면 아무 테이블에라도 앉을 수 없나요?

Waiter: 죄송하지만 예약이 꽉 찼습니다. 한 시간 뒤에 다시 오실 수 있나요?

Client: 그래요. 그러면 한 시간 뒤에 올게요.

Waiter: 예약을 하시겠습니까?

Client: 아니요, 그냥 이따가 제 운을 한번 시험해 볼게요.

Waiter: 알겠습니다. 이따 뵙겠습니다.

Scene 7

Film dialogue and vocabulary   p. 58-60

C: 아빠가 애지중지하는 그림들을 모아둔 방이에요. 세상에서 가장 아끼시는 거죠.

O: 보고 싶어요!

C: 아버지가 아무도 못 들어가게 해요! 들어가려면 비밀번호를 알아야 하죠.

O: 하지만 똑똑하니까 알 거 아니에요.

M: 웬 친구니, 커티스?

C: 아빠, 어제 런던에 가신 줄 알았는데요.

M: 안 갔어. 로버트 머리입니다. 그냥 로버트라고 불러요.

O: 올리브 그린이에요. 반갑습니다. 머리 씨… 로버트!

M: 커티스, 손님에게 내 그림을 보여주려고 했구나. 좋아. 다 같이 보는 게 어떨까? (…)

C: 엄마예요. 전 전화 좀…

M: 가서 받거라, 아들. 손님은 내가 접대하고 있을 테니까. "엉겅퀴"… 프레데리크 보몽의 걸작이죠. 최고의 인상파 화가라는 평가를 받고 있어요. 그가 이 그림을 그릴 당시인 1880년에는…

O: 1879년요. 고고학 전공이거든요. 이쪽에 관심이 많죠.

M: 올리브, 커티스의 다른 애인들과는 다르군요. 대부분 우아하고 똑똑한 척하는데 아가씨는 멍청한 속물인 척하는군요. 왜 그러는 거죠?

`flirt with Murray`

O: 커티스 때문에 온 게 아닐지도 모르죠.

M: 그렇다면… 그런 경우라면, 똑똑한 미국인 아가씨…

C: 미안해요, 올리브. 처리해야 할 일이 생겼어요. 시내까지 태워드릴까요?

O: 네, 그래요.

`show surprise`

O: 무슨 말씀이신지 모르겠는데요!

M: 아는 것 같은데요, 그린 씨!

C: 미안해요, 올리브. 처리해야 할 일이 생겼어요. 시내까지 태워드릴까요?

O: 네, 그래요.

M: 머리일세. 어떤 여자 뒷조사 좀 해줘야겠어. 미국인이야. 이름은 올리브 그린…

`Communication situations` p. 64~65

Olive: 머리 씨… 어… 로버트! 구경시켜 주셔서 감사해요. 당신의 집은 정말 영국 귀족의 오래된 저택이군요.

`Dialogue 1`

Murray: 맞아요. 19세기에 지어졌죠.

Olive: 이곳에 침실 25개, 예배당, 식당, 그리고 연회장이 있다는 게 사실인가요?

Murray: 서재도 잊지 말아요.

Olive: 서재요! 저는 그런 공간을 좋아해요. 저도 볼 수 있을까요?

Murray: 물론이죠. 이쪽으로 와요.

Olive: 와! 굉장하네요. 그리고 그림도 있고요. 이곳이 그 유명한 당신의 화랑인가요?
Murray: 아뇨. 제 화랑은 그것보다 훨씬 더 넓고 더 진귀하답니다…
Olive: 그렇다면 정말 멋지겠네요. 무척 보고 싶어요, 로버트.
Murray: 아무한테나 보여주진 않지만 미소가 정말 아름다우셔서…
Olive: 정말 영광이에요. 아시겠지만 당신의 화랑에 얽힌 전설이 있잖아요.
Murray: 무슨 전설요?
Olive: 음, 사람들은 당신이 수집품을 위해 걸작을 훔친다고 하더군요.
Murray: 질투가 나서 그러는 거죠.
Olive: 네, 분명 그럴 거예요.

Dialogue 2

Murray: 음, 증조부께서 19세기에 지으셨지요.
Olive: 잠깐만요. 캠벨 저택이라고 불리잖아요, 머리 저택이 아니라.
Murray: 똑똑하시군요. 제가 한 방 먹었네요.
Olive: 그러면 진짜 이야기는 무엇인가요, 로버트?
Murray: 제 친척이 지었는데 베아트리스가 샀지요.
Olive: 로버트, 지금 저를 놀리시는 거군요! 하지만 괜찮아요. 여기서 당신이 가장 좋아하는 장소는 어디인가요?
Murray: 제 차고예요.
Olive: 벤틀리 자동차 컬렉션 때문인가요?
Murray: 네, 가장 오래된 차는 1920년식이죠.
Olive: 상당히 인상 깊군요. 타 볼 수 있을까요?

Dialogue 3

Murray: 이쪽으로 오세요.
Olive: 저 문은요? 어디로 통하나요?
Murray: 제 사무실로요.
Olive: 제가 볼 수 있을까요?
Murray: 안 돼요!
Olive: 흠, 다급하게 대답하시니 호기심이 생기네요. 저 안에 뭘 숨기고 있는지 궁금해요.

Scene 8

Film dialogue and vocabulary p. 68~69

울타리는… 쉽다.

뚫고 들어가면 된다. 넘어가도 되지만, 문제는 감시 카메라다…

해킹을 할 수 있지만, 아니… 그건 너무 위험해!

캠벨 저택을 가로질러 흐르는 냇물이 있다. 거기엔 카메라가 없어.

헤엄쳐 들어가면 되지만…

아니! 내가 무슨 제임스 본드도 아니고!

어떻게 사람들 눈에 안 띄고 건물로 들어가지? 더 중요한 건…

어떻게 눈에 안 띄고 나와서 탈출하지?

O: 커티스, 무슨 일이에요?

C: 올리브.

C: 아직 안 자서 다행이에요. 저기, 내일 저녁에 우리 집에서 성대한 자선 파티를 해요. 아주 지루한 행사인데… 지루한 사람들이 많이 오죠.

O: 불쌍하네요. 정말 안됐어요!

C: 나랑 같이 가지 않을래요? 그럼… 난 재미있을 것 같은데요.

O: 좋아요! 갈게요.

Communication situations   p. 72~73

Olive: 안녕! 잘 있니? 오늘 하루 어떻게 보내고 있어?

Dialogue 1

Alfie: 안녕 올리브. 나는 좋아, 고마워, 너는?

Olive: 나도 괜찮아, 고마워. 요즘 어떻게 지내?

Alfie: 음, 집에만 틀어박혀 있어.

Olive: 무슨 일 있어?

Alfie: 묻지도 마.

Olive: 아, 그러지 말고. 나한테는 말해도 돼. 안 웃을 게, 약속해.

Alfie: 다리가 부러졌어.

Olive: 다리? 어쩌다 그랬어?

Alfie: 사다리에 올라 커튼을 달려고 하는데…

Olive: 알았어, 알았어, 나머지는 알고 싶지 않아! 그러면 내일 콘서트는 못 가겠네?

Alfie: 아냐, 아냐, 갈 수 있어!

Olive: 갈 수 있다고? 정말? 부러진 다리로? 아, 제발, 말도 안 되는 소리 하지 마!

Dialogue 2

Alfie: 여보세요! 여보세요? 안 들려요. 다시 한번 말씀해 주시겠어요?

Olive: 응, 여보세요. 나 올리브야.

Alfie: 이제야 들리는군. 어떻게 지내?

Olive: 잘 지내, 고마워. 록 콘서트 티켓 두 장이 생겨서 전화했어. 너도 갈래?

Alfie: 장난해? 당연히 가야지!

Olive: 콘서트는 9월 5일이야. 오후 8시에 시작이고.

Alfie: 완벽하네. 내가 6시 45분에 데리러 갈게.

Olive: 좋아. 그럼 6시 45분에 보자.

Dialogue 3

Alfie: 안녕 올리브, 무슨 일이야?

Olive: 안녕, 주말 계획을 물어보려고 전화했어. 혹시 할 일 있니?

Alfie: 음, 일요일에는 가족을 만날 건데 토요일에는 한가해.

Olive: 그렇구나. 흠, 나 토요일 아침에 조깅하러 가려고 해. 나랑 같이 갈래?

Alfie: 제정신이야? 나 조깅 싫어하잖아.

Olive: 그래, 알았어. 괜찮아. 다음에 다른 일로 만나지 뭐.

Dialogue 4

Alfie: 영화관에 가려고 해.

Olive: 멋진 계획 같은데. 같이 갈래?

Alfie: 음, 안 될 것 없지.

Olive: 좋아. 영화관에서 7시 45분에 보자.

Alfie: 그래. 내가 늦으면 표 좀 끊어줘.

Olive: 알았어, 그럴게.

Scene 9

Film dialogue and vocabulary   p. 76~77

O: 밤에 외출할 때 입을 멋진 옷을 찾는데요.

S: 밤에 외출한다는 게 술집에 가는 건가요?

O: 아뇨. 왕실의 친구들과 함께 공식 만찬에 갈 거예요.

S: 음, 그렇군요… 그렇다면 제대로 찾아오셨네요. 온갖 종류의 드레스가 다 있거든요.

O: 정말요?

S: 아뇨, 없어요. 올드 베리에서는 여자들이 드레스를 안 사요. 미안해요.

insist

O: 왠지 모르게 그 말을 못 믿겠네요. 우리 함께 좋은 옷을 찾아볼까요? (…)

O: 저 옷… 예쁘네요. 왜 진작 얘기 안 했어요?

S: 그게, 제가 살을 빼는 중이에요. 매일 이 드레스를 보면서 속으로 말하죠. "이거 입을 만큼 날씬했으면!" 하지만 보시다시피…

O: 이걸로 할게요.

leave

S: 와 봐요. 어울릴 만한 옷이 있어요.

O: 저 옷… 예쁘네요. 왜 진작 얘기 안 했어요?

S: 그게, 제가 살을 빼는 중이에요. 매일 이 드레스를 보면서 속으로 말하죠. "이거 입을 만큼 날씬했으면!" 하지만 보시다시피…

O: 이걸로 할게요.

Communication situations   p. 82~84

Shop assistant: 안녕하세요, 도와드릴까요?

Dialogue 1

Client: 네, 해리 포터를 찾고 있는데요.

Shop assistant: 하지만 이곳은 서점이 아니에요! 신문 가판대죠. 저희는 신문, 잡지, 티슈, 전화 카드를 판매해요…

Client: 아, 죄송해요.

Shop assistant: 괜찮습니다. 제가 서점이 어디에 있는지 알려 드릴게요. 저 제과점 보이세요?

Client: 네, 보여요.

Shop assistant: 서점은 제과점 건너편에 있어요.

Client: 아 그렇군요, 이제야 보이네요.

Shop assistant: 바로 그거예요. 좋은 하루 보내세요!

Dialogue 2

Client: 네, 뭔가 멋진 것을 찾고 있어요.

Shop assistant: 그러시군요. 신발, 바지, 셔츠, 아니면 드레스 중 어떤 것으로 보시나요?

Client: 새 신발 한 켤레를 사고 싶어요.

Shop assistant: 신발 코너는 2층에 있습니다. 저를 따라오세요. 어떤 종류의 신발을 찾으세요?

Client: 가죽 부츠 좀 보고 싶어요.

Shop assistant: 알겠습니다. 무슨 색상으로요?

Client: 검은색요. 그리고 신발 끈이 없고 지퍼만 있는 것으로요.

Shop assistant: 죄송하지만, 신발 끈이 없는 신발은 없습니다.

> Dialogue 3

Client: 아, 네. 이 청바지가 다른 색으로도 있나요?

Shop assistant: 물론이죠. 검은색과 파란색 중 어떤 것이 좋으세요?

Client: 파란색요.

(...)

Shop assistant: 바지는 괜찮으세요?

Client: 10은 너무 꽉 끼네요. 더 큰 치수가 필요해요.

Shop assistant: 알겠습니다. 여기 있어요.

Client: 고마워요. 얼마죠?

Shop assistant: 56파운드예요. 그리고 계산대는 저쪽에 있습니다.

> Dialogue 4

Client: 네, 뭔가 멋진 것을 찾고 있어요.

Shop assistant: 그러시군요. 신발, 바지, 셔츠, 아니면 드레스 중 어떤 것으로 보시나요?

Client: 바지요. 음, 청바지요. 정확히 말하면.

Shop assistant: 알겠습니다. 치수가 어떻게 되세요? 10 입으세요, 12 입으세요?

Client: 잘 모르겠어요.

Shop assistant: 둘 다 가져다드릴게요. 여기 있습니다. 탈의실은 저쪽에 있습니다.

Scene 10

Film dialogue and vocabulary   p. 86-87

C: 이쪽은 올리브. 올리브, 저희 어머니예요.

O: 어머니한테 마실 것 좀 갖다 드릴래요?

B: 올리브, 커티스에겐 두 부류의 여자가 달라붙어요. 첫 번째는 저 아이보다도 더 멍청한 부류예요. 상처만 받고 버려지는 여자들이죠. 다른 부류는 커티스보다 똑똑하고 돈 때문에 걔를 이용해 먹으려는 여자들이죠. 사랑하는 제 남편이 그런 여자들을 떼어내는 데 소질이 있죠! 하지만 당신은… 남편이 당신한테 관심이 있어요. 남편이 생각하는 것 이상으로 당신이 똑똑한 거겠죠. 올리브, 저이는 당신을 행복하게 해 주지 못해요. 그의 돈도 당신을 행복하게 해 주지 못해요. 내가 누구보다 잘 알아요.

C: 도와줘요! … 도와주세요!

O: 젠장, 예쁜 드레스였는데!

O: 정말 미안해요, 커티스. 어머니께 안부 전해줘요.

Communication situations p. 90~91

Olive: 안녕, 잘 지내? 아, 좀 걱정 있는 얼굴이네. 무슨 일 있어?

Dialogue 1

Alfie: 안녕, 걱정은 없어. 그냥 몸이 좋지 않을 뿐이야.
Olive: 그러게, 안쓰러워 보이는구나.
Alfie: 어, 정말 고마워
Olive: 열이 높아?
Alfie: 아니, 하지만 기침은 해.
Olive: 기침약을 먹으면 이틀 뒤에 괜찮아질 거야.

Dialogue 2

Alfie: 아, 우리 아빠 때문이야.
Olive: 왜? 아버지께 문제라도 있어?
Alfie: 음, 아버지의 혈액 검사 결과가 안 좋아.
Olive: 아, 걱정되겠구나.
Alfie: 그렇기는 한데 놀랍지는 않아.
Olive: 무슨 뜻이야?
Alfie: 음, 우리 아빠의 생활 방식을 봐. 우선, 애연가잖아.
Olive: 내가 의사는 아니지만, 이게 흡연 탓은 아닌 것 같은데.
Alfie: 식사도 정크푸드만 잔뜩 드시고. 도움이 안 되지.
Olive: 아, 그러면 다 지방 때문인가 보다. 채식을 해 보셔야겠네.
Alfie: 우리 아빠가 퍽이나 채식을?
Olive: 그러면 균형 잡힌 식사라도 시도해 보시면 어떨까? 괜찮은 영양사를 만나 보시면 좋겠다.

Dialogue 3

Alfie: 안녕. 음, 남동생이 걱정돼.
Olive: 무슨 일 있어?
Alfie: 걔가 식중독에 걸린 것 같아.
Olive: 왜 그렇게 생각해?
Alfie: 음, 증상을 보면…
Olive: 증상이 어떤데?
Alfie: 토할 뿐만 아니라 열도 높고 배도 아프대.
Olive: 아, 그러면 네 말이 맞을 수도 있겠다. 의사를 불러야겠네. 탈수는 아주 심각한 문제일 수 있으니까.

Translation

Dialogue 4

Alfie: 맞아. 몸이 떨려.

Olive: 열도 나니?

Alfie: 응, 오한이 날 때면 늘 열이나.

Olive: 아, 안타깝구나. 머리나 목도 아파?

Alfie: 모든 증상을 다 겪고 있어. 오한, 고열, 두통에다가 목도 아파.

Olive: 병원에 가 봐야겠네.

Alfie: 지금 가는 길이야.

Olive: 행운을 빌고 어서 낫기를 바라!

Scene 11

Film dialogue and vocabulary p. 94~95

O: 잠금장치를 해제했어요. 들어왔어요.

O: 그림 앞이에요. 이제 내가⋯

C: 올리브, 잠깐! 계획이 변경됐소.

O: 뭐라고요? 미쳤어요?

C: 그림 뒤에 비밀 금고가 있소. 그 금고를 열고 안에 든 서류를 가져오시오.

O: 얘기가 다르잖아요! 그럴 시간이 없어요!

C: 시키는 대로 해! 안 그러면 캘리포니아 산페르난도의 어머니 주소를 커쉬에게 알릴 테니까. 커쉬가 당신은 못 건드려도 당신 어머니를 죽이면 기분이 나아질지도 모르지.

Bodyguard: 그림은 안 훔쳐갔습니다!

M: 올리브, 아직 파티장을 안 떠나서 다행이야⋯ 가이, 수갑 채워!

M: 꼼짝 마, 아니면 쏘겠어!

Communication situations p. 100~101

Assistant: 드디어 5월이네요. 저희가 행사 시장에 들어온 지 반년째인데, 여름은 우리의 능력을 충분히 발휘할 기회입니다!

Dialogue 1

Boss: 좋아요. 그러면 행사 신청 마감일 전체 목록을 작성해 줄래요?

Assistant: 이미 해 두었습니다.

Boss: 정말이요? 대단하군요!

Assistant: 우선 LIFT 페스티벌이 6월에 있고, 그다음에는 캠던 페스티벌이 7월에 있고, 노팅힐 카니발이 8월 하순에 있습니다.

Boss: 전부 신청하세요.

Assistant: 정말이요? 저 행사들 모두 준비하는 데 시간이 꽤 많이 걸립니다만.

Boss: 음, 이름을 알리려면 목표를 높게 잡아야죠.

Assistant: 그게 맞는지는 시간이 지나면 알게 되겠죠.

Dialogue 2

Boss: 업무 회의에서 우리가 논의했던 행사들에 대해 저에게 메모 좀 작성해 줄래요?

Assistant: 물론입니다. 언제 드리면 될까요?

Boss: 메모에 대해 논의할 수 있을 때 알려 주세요.

Assistant: 제가 특히 집중할 사항이 있을까요?

Boss: 규모가 크고, 국제적인 공연예술 축제에 집중해 주세요.

Assistant: 에든버러 페스티벌 같은 것을 말씀하시는 건가요?

Boss: 네, 그게 바로 제가 생각하는 거예요!

Assistant: 알겠습니다. 일단 다문화 행사의 목록을 만드는 것부터 시작해서 어떻게 흘러갈지 한번 보죠.

Dialogue 3

Boss: 제가 기억하기로는 미술 전시회가 6월에, 콘서트는 7월에 열리죠.

Assistant: 네, 맞습니다.

Boss: 먼저 전시회를 처리해 봅시다.

Assistant: 그런데 우리가 뭘 전시할 예정이죠, 그림인가요, 조각인가요? 결정하셨나요?

Boss: 네, 결정했어요. 조각전을 할 예정이에요.

Assistant: 그러면 그다음엔 뭘 하면 되죠?

Boss: 예술가들 그리고 시의회 의원들과 회의를 잡아 주세요.

Assistant: 이 회의의 주제는 무엇이 될까요?

Boss: 좋은 질문이에요. 먼저 안건을 준비하세요.

Assistant: 그렇게 하겠습니다. 하지만 발송하기 전에 한번 검토해 주셨으면 하는데, 괜찮으시죠?

Boss: 우선은 장소, 날짜, 그리고 시의회의 보조금을 포함하세요.

Assistant: 알겠습니다, 그렇게 하겠습니다.

Scene 12

Film dialogue and vocabulary   p. 104~105

M: 안타깝군, 올리브. 좋은 친구가 되길 바랐는데.
D: 총 버려요!
M: 오언 순경, 저 여자를 체포하게! 아주 중요한 사업 서류를 훔쳤다네.
D: 머리 씨, 총 버려요! 어서요!
M: 위험한 범죄자일세! 내 직원들을 공격하고 아들에게 약을 먹였어.
D: 올리브, 그랬어요?

D: 신고해야 해요. 우리가 한 짓은… 난 이러면 안 돼요! 난 경찰이라고요!
O: 데이비드, 진정해요!
D: 올리브, 대체 정체가 뭐예요? 이름이 올리브가 맞기는 해요? 정말 범죄자예요?
O: 차는 어디에 뒀어요? 네, 데이비드. 난 범죄자예요. 난 미술품을 훔쳐요. 가끔 사람들을 해치긴 하지만 절대 죽이진 않아요.
D: 그럼 나는요? 나는 왜 끌어들인 거죠?
O: 문제는 내가 당신을 좋아한다는 거예요, 데이비드. 누군가를 이렇게 좋아하긴 오랜만이에요. 그래서 곤란하게 만들고 싶지 않았어요.

Communication situations   p. 110~111

Man: 이봐, 나는 운전하면서, 도로 표지판도 보면서 지도까지 읽고 있어. 네가 하는 말까지 일일이 신경 쓸 겨를은 없다고.

Dialogue 1

Woman: 그럼 내비게이션을 켜.
Man: 이 기기는 못 미더워. 멍청하거든.
Woman: 나도 지금 너한테 똑같은 말을 할 수 있을 것 같아.
Man: 믿기 힘들겠지만 도로 공사가 진행 중일 때는, 기기가 이상해진단 말이야.
Woman: 하지만 해 보지도 않았잖아!
Man: 할 필요도 없고 할 생각도 없어.
Woman: 가끔 넌 참 속이 좁은 것 같아, 알아?
Man: 아니, 그렇지 않아. 나는 그저… 흠, 그저 나만의 원칙을 고수할 뿐이지.

Dialogue 2

Woman: 알았어. 계속 운전해, 나는 도로 표지판 공부하면서 운전면허 딸 준비나 하고 있을 테니까.

Man: 정말 좋은 생각이네. 시작해 보자. 이 표지판은 무슨 뜻이지?

Woman: 어떤 표지판?

Man: 빨간색 원인데 바탕은 흰색이고 검은색 기호가 있는 것.

Woman: 음, 안에 숫자가 있으면 그건 제한 속도를 나타내.

Man: 좋아. 그런데 거기에 선이 그어져 있으면?

Woman: 제한 속도가 더는 유효하지 않은 거지.

Man: 잘했어!

Dialogue 3

Woman: 그러면 길가에 차를 세우고 저쪽에 주차하자.

Man: 왜?

Woman: 시내 중심가에 도착했는데 차로는 더 들어갈 수가 없어.

Man: 아. 그렇구나. 그러면 어떻게 관광을 하지?

Woman: 지하철이 가장 빠를 것 같은데.

Man: 첫째, 여기서는 '전철'이라고 불러, 그리고 둘째, 전철에서는 아무것도 보이지 않을 거야.

Woman: 맞아… 그러면 버스를 제안하지.

Man: 그래, 알았다, 줄 서 보는 경험을 해 보고 싶은 거구나.

Woman: 응, 그리고 기사님에게 표도 사 보고.

Man: 넌 이상해. 하지만 좋아, 그러지 뭐. 버스를 타자.

memo

Olive Green